HEROES
AND
VILLAINS

*An Anthology of
Animosity and Admiration*

Introduced by John Walsh

VICTOR GOLLANCZ
in association with
THE INDEPENDENT MAGAZINE
LONDON

First published in Great Britain 1994
by Victor Gollancz Ltd
A Division of the Cassell group
Villiers House, 41/47 Strand, London WC2N 5JE

Copyright © Newspaper Publishing plc 1994
Copyright in individual pieces © individual authors

The right of the individual authors to be identified
as authors of their work has been asserted by them
in accordance with the Copyright, Designs and
Patents Act, 1988

A catalogue record for this book is
available from the British Library

ISBN 0 575 05839 0

Grateful acknowledgement is made to the following for
permission to reproduce illustrations: Alexandra Burke
(David Baddiel, p. 11), Popperfoto (Joe Orton, p. 15, Jake
Thackray, p. 131), The Hulton Deutsch Collection
(Rasputin, p. 19, Edgar Allen Poe, p. 23, the Pope, p. 71,
Barbara Cartland, p. 83, Albert Pierrepoint, p. 87, Samuel
Beckett, p. 103, Aleister Crowley, p. 127, Bernard
Manning, p. 157, Colette, p. 177, Eugene Terre'Blanche,
p. 181, the Singing Postman, p. 197, Pamella Bordes,
p. 205), Glyn Satterley (John Byrne, p. 47), Antonia Fraser
(Mother Ignatius, p. 95), Charles Hopkinson (Nick Hornby,
p. 123), Mary Evans Picture Library (Bach, p. 147), Joanne
O'Brien (Ralph Steadman, p. 193), the National Gallery
(Jesus, p. 221)

Photoset in Great Britain by
Rowland Phototypesetting Ltd, Bury St Edmunds, Suffolk
Printed and bound in Great Britain by
Guernsey Press Co. Ltd, Guernsey, Channel Isles

INTRODUCTION

by John Walsh

Heroes and Villains has been a regular feature of *The Independent Magazine* since its first issue of 20 August 1988. After an uncertain start – the earliest contributions were as-told-to reports or personal histories of multiple fan-worship – the column crystallised into the form we know today with Beryl Bainbridge's witty appreciation of Rasputin ('I think of him as a breath of rank air') on 10 September. The column was then called My Hero, and dealt only in appreciation, praise or would-be empathy. A year of positive thinking later, its brief was widened to include bursts of accusation, malice and disaffection under the heading of Villains. Its success was enduring: over three hundred heroes and villains have been memorialised or trashed in the last six years, and it has never been hard to coax contributions from eminent celebrities. Sometimes, indeed, it has seemed as though an invitation to nominate a hero or villain in the pages of the *Magazine* is counted as a marker on the tally-stick of distinction, just as an invitation to appear on *Desert Island Discs* suggests that your career may not have been entirely without success.

In this collection, we reprint the best contributions to the three hundred. What characterises, and justifies, this selection is the attention paid in each to the concept of heroism or villainy, as a personal response to another's behaviour. Some

3

lesser would-be contributors have made the fatal error of choosing an admirable (or obnoxious) figure from history, delivering a potted, encyclopaedia-entry account of their life and work, and tacking a moral judgement on at the end. This approach might have satisfied the ancient Greeks, from whom the word 'hero' – meaning a man of superhuman qualities, favoured by the gods – derives; but it is of no consequence in our godless, post-Freudian world. A choice of hero or villain should tell us as much about the writer as about the object of his or her attention.

My own views on the subject were settled quite early in life, when I was given a copy of Charles Kingsley's *The Heroes* by a well-meaning family friend. The book told you all you needed to know about Hercules and the Augean Stables, Theseus and the Minotaur, Perseus and his flying horse, and impressed me without making me feel even momentarily starstruck. Even in short trousers, I knew they couldn't be real heroes because the exploits for which they were so celebrated – spring-cleaning a sewer, negotiating a maze and beheading a snake-infested witch – were impossible to replicate in the real world. My own objects of admiration in those pre-teen years – Donald Campbell, Albert Schweitzer, Captain Hurricane (of *Valiant* comic), Peter Bonetti (the Chelsea goalkeeper), Napoleon Solo (of *The Man From U.N.C.L.E.*) and a whole raft of rock stars – were people into whose heroic behaviour patterns I could, I imagined, effortlessly fit, given the right circumstances.

It's quite an imaginative leap – the leap that, say, John Lennon's killer Mark Chapman failed to make – to allow your heroes to have a life of their own, outside your desire to turn into them. The next step is to domesticate your admiration, such that you imagine having a relationship with them. Roddy Doyle's boyish conviction (page 77) that he and Charlie Cooke would become friends ('He'd be a big brother to me. I'd clean his boots. We'd share digs. My mother would like him. He'd come to our house for Christmas because his parents were dead. I'd save his life. He'd come to my funeral') must strike a plangent chord in many hero-worshipping hearts. Perhaps the final condition of fandom is to admit that actually to meet one's hero in the flesh would be to die a little: to have it confirmed that the god-like figure of your imaginative projections is human after all – smaller than you'd thought, considerably older, strikingly uninspired in conversation and, worst of all, wholly uninterested in meeting you. Believe me, I know: I've met Mick Jagger.

Perhaps the most striking feature of the heroes and villains featured in these pages is their heterogeneity. A more motley (indeed a more unlikely) throng could hardly be imagined. One thinks of Thomas Carlyle and his 1840 lecture series On Hero-worship and the Heroic in History, in which the great moralist identified six categories in which great men might be found: the Hero as Divinity, the Hero as Prophet, the Hero as Poet, the Hero as Priest, the Hero as Man of Letters and the Hero as King. Few of his categorical supermen survive into the Nineties: no kings, no prophets, no priests (unless you count the Pope, in Richard Dawkins's tongue-in-cheek eulogy), only one poet (and Carlyle would *not* have approved of Tom Pickard) and one divinity – A. N. Wilson's revisionist portrait of a distinctly worldly Jesus Christ.

There are, however, still lots of men, and women, of letters, revealing how much the worship of the secular written word has superseded that of the spiritual in the last

150 years. And alongside them sits a whole new Dewey system of odd classifications. The Hero as Singer (Billy Fury, Elvis, Jake Thackray), the Hero as Cartoon Character (Bluto), the Hero as Footballer (Perry Groves, Gazza, Cooke) or Dancer (Fred Astaire) or Sexual Conman (Frank Harris). The heroine as Wrestler (Klondyke Kate) or Prostitute (Pamella Bordes) or Soap Opera Star (Noele Gordon) . . . One imagines Thomas Carlyle revolving slowly in Paradise, his slumbers plagued by awful dreams.

The Villain pieces, it will soon be apparent, are in the minority in this collection. Though they are sometimes more amusing to read than goody-goody dilations on heroism, they tend to lack the personal touch, the swoon factor, that sense of private appropriation that is apparent in the phrase 'My hero'. But no one reading Joan Smith's hatchet job on Lord Young, or Dennis Potter's excoriation of Ira B. Sankey, or Antony Sher's appalled fascination with Eugene Terre'Blanche, could doubt that personal, fundamentalist rage is as available to western sensibilities as enlightened admiration.

So read and enjoy – and you will find yourself surprisingly moved at times. For human beings are invariably found at their most sincere when discussing people rather than things or ideas. And in celebrating or deprecating the lives and productions and voices and achievements of those who mean most to us, we reveal the best, or at least the most interesting, parts of ourselves. This collection seeks only to entertain; but the impulses that led its contributors to their thousand-word conclusions clearly sprang straight from the heart.

GILBERT ADAIR

◊

Fred Astaire

29 June 1991

The novelist and critic Gilbert Adair applauds the nonchalant perfection of Fred Astaire

I fell in love with Fred Astaire at first sight. I was seven years old (or rather, as I would insist with childish pedantry, seven and a half), the year was 1952 and the film in question was *Royal Wedding*, which my grandmother took me to see because the wedding of the title was that of our very own Princess Elizabeth to Philip Mountbatten. It wasn't, as I now know, one of Astaire's best, but its highlight was an unforgettable sequence which had him, in the suite of a London hotel, dancing first on the floor, then over the furniture, then, as nonchalantly as if he were stepping off a kerb, leaping sideways on to one of the bedroom walls and sashaying upside-down across the ceiling.

Although a precociously well-informed film buff for a seven-and-a-half-year-old, I knew nothing of special effects and thus believed that Fred Astaire *really could dance on the ceiling*. And even the expertise that I've since come to acquire, the realisation that such an effect is achieved by simultaneously tilting the camera and the set, has in no way dented my conviction that in Fred Astaire's case technical artifice was unnecessary.

The snag with love at first sight is that it seldom extends to the second. Yet, with the passing years, with, indeed, the passing decades, and whatever my shifting allegiances in matters filmic, I've never ceased to think of Fred Astaire as one of those supernaturally gifted individuals for whose sake the cinema exists; who are, in a sense, *better* than the cinema. For he impresses me not just as a dancer (even if he was, by pretty much universal accord, one of the greatest of the century), not just as a singer, actor and peerlessly debonair light comedian, but, above all, as the epitome of style – style in the sense implied in Buffon's '*Le style est l'homme même*', style as a *heraldic* quality, bearing the same relation to conventional attributes of stylishness as the lions and wolves rampant on coats-of-arms bear to real animals. Astaire might have personified Style in the niche of a medieval cathedral as other idealised forms personified Chastity and Avarice.

The external expression of this style was of course vestimentary as much as choreographic, and its primary signifier was the top hat, white tie and tails that he wore in the films for which he's still best remembered, those in which he and Ginger Rogers danced together like two porcelain figurines endlessly revolving on the lid of a music box. In a tuxedo Astaire struck one as so pristinely, flawlessly chic it was as if a conjuror had miraculously pulled him, like a white rabbit, from out of his own top hat. So irresistible was his own personal 'look' it seemed to radiate out from him and determine the overall visual tonality of his films (whose directors' names are rarely cited by critics writing about them). And *Top Hat*, *Swing Time*, *The Gay Divorcee*, *Shall We Dance?* and *Follow the Fleet* – all those euphoric musicals in which Astaire and Rogers ingenuously defied the goose-step that was sweeping Europe with the Yam and the Carioca – were so rigorously designed for black-and-white cinematography that 'colourising' them (and it has been tried) would be as nonsensical as colourising a tux.

Such monochromatic colour-coding, so to speak, worked on several levels at once. There was, first of all, the crisp black-and-white ensemble, like that of a svelte penguin, presented by Astaire himself. Then there was the black of Astaire's tailcoat as it juxtaposed the filmy white of Rogers's gown. And, finally, there was the jet black of a patently artificial scene-painter's sky as glimpsed from the french window of the films' typically all-white, Syrie Maughamish décors –

décors that always made me think of the inside of a two-tiered wedding cake.

Maybe precisely because she was a good, but not great, dancer, Rogers fitted her partner like a glove. She contrived to humanise him, sexualise him, frustrate his occasionally rather nerve-racking tendency to inhuman, asexual perfection (whereas the classily statuesque Cyd Charisse, who was more nearly in his league, came across as slightly stiff in his arms). The difference between them, that which makes Rogers stylish but Astaire the very embodiment of Style, can actually be demonstrated with a video recorder, a freeze-frame button and a tape of one of their films. Where Rogers may at times seem klunky, even flat-footed, Astaire, at no matter what point of a dance routine the image is arrested, will be transfixed in a pose of supreme elegance, shrugging his feet as casually as if they were his shoulders, and displaying, at the choreography's transitional stages, none of those minor gestural infelicities, mostly imperceptible to the naked eye, to which one imagined even the greatest dancers had to be prone.

And that, ultimately, is why he has become so important to me. Perfection – which is, after all, what every dancer, every writer, every artist, aspires to – is almost always a matter of *trompe l'oeil*. Look closely, and you can't help noticing the cracks, the flaws, the tiny, nagging clues reminding you that even perfectionists nod. But, as video proves, Astaire never nodded, perhaps could not, because, in his case, style really did make the man, because what he possessed was not 'a style' but style itself.

In fact, what I have to say about him can be put in just ten words: I would like to write the way Fred Astaire danced.

DAVID BADDIEL

◇

Paul Gascoigne

4 December 1993

*David Baddiel on the moment when
Paul Gascoigne changed from being a
villain to being a hero*

The only heroes I have are footballers. People for whom I have the greatest respect and admiration – John Updike, Eric Morecambe, Steven Spielberg – but who are not footballers cannot inspire in me the feeling, the heroic feeling: a kind of tearful awe. As a writer, Updike may truly have captured the desperate internality of the modern soul; but until he cleaves Brewer United's back four in half with a forty-yard pass, he shan't transport me. I shan't gasp: *My hero*. Footballers have this over other artists; it allows them not to bother about the majority of their personality. A footballer can be the most bigoted, insensitive philistine, but let him break the back of the net from well outside the box and I cannot stop my hands from clasping instinctively together in an attitude of total worship. It doesn't matter if he's the biggest prat in the world: and here we come to Paul Gascoigne.

Really, he should be a villain. Consider the list of sins: the unfunny funny faces, the 'Fog on the Tyne' and 'Geordie Boys' raps, having a best friend called Five Bellies – these lapses of taste alone should be enough to consign him to the cultural scrapheap somewhere between Paul Daniels and Black Lace. I mean, imagine for a second, Gazza, if he wasn't an astonishing footballer – what an irritating twat he'd be; and if he wasn't a footballer at all, how easily he'd fit among the whiteshirts singing, 'Get your tits out for the lads' in the seventh circle of hell this country calls nightclubs. And yet he redeems it, he redeems it all with every ball borne across the grass on angels' wings. He more than redeems it, he transmogrifies it; all that bollocks becomes something else in the context of the football, it becomes the manure out of which grows the sunflower, because the fact is that if Gazza wasn't such a prat he wouldn't be such a player. The only other regular England player – which leaves out, through tears, the Welsh Ryan Giggs and the scandalously uncapped Matthew Le Tissier – who could possibly be said to have the same kind of natural ability is John Barnes. But Barnes can't perform like Gascoigne at international level, because Barnes has a brain, because he has enough intelligence to be self-conscious: therein lies his paralysis, in the space left over in his mind to thinking What if I should look like an idiot? This is clearly not a thought that could ever occur to Paul Gascoigne – luckily, for in that vacuum of self-awareness lies the spark of abandon, the wanton ability to try the extravagant, to try the ridiculous, and to see it come off.

There was, of course, one moment when Gazza did genuinely, in a classical sense, become a hero. In Aristotle's *Poetics*, the definition of a tragic hero is given as 'a prince, beloved of his nation-state, who, at the moment of his greatest potential, comes to disaster by his own undoing'. Most contemporary thinkers believe that this mythical idea of tragic heroism, with its ordered structure of rise and fall, and its implicit belief in a universal justice, is conceptually untenable in our nihilistic, chaos-ridden modernity. Such men and such narratives just do not happen any more. I watched Gazza crash knee-first into Gary Charles in the opening five minutes of the 1991 FA Cup Final and thought: Yes, they do. If the Jacobean playwright John Webster had written *The Most High Tragedie of Paul Gascoyne, The Foot Baller* in May 1991, he'd hardly have had to elaborate on his source material: the hero, a mixture of genius and clown, becomes the object of a nation's love, then, at the high point of the turning wheel, goes mad, and commits suicide on the public stage. At the high point of the turning wheel; there's the rub. If Gascoigne had destroyed himself at any

13

other moment, except five minutes into the FA Cup Final, his narrative would not have so borne the mark of destiny. It made me wonder if there wasn't a higher power at work here: if Gazza's story, in its classical neatness, didn't prove the existence of God.

Now, I have to be honest here. I wrote this piece sixteen months ago, just after Gascoigne had started playing again. And, then, the last paragraph went like this:

'And now, now that he's come back, it still seems like a story, not just a jumble of disconnected events. Of course you want him to be even more outstanding than before, but he won't be, surely, that only happens in books – but then you remember the forty-five-yard goal against Arsenal and Barry Davies saying, "This is – oh, this is *Boys' Own* stuff!", and you begin to hope, and then he scores, he scores on his return for Lazio against Tottenham, and so you hope some more, and then he plays like a god against Norway, and so, despite everything, despite Graham Taylor, despite what a mess your life is, you think that perhaps there is somewhere a universe with beginnings, middles and ends after all. And in this case, brilliantly, an epilogue.'

A paragraph brimming with hope; but then Gazza blew it like he did once before – with a booking. So he didn't play in Rotterdam, and Taylor, secretly pleased, his donkey soul allergic with bitterness at seeing someone dance with the ball, put in *Carlton Palmer*. Which means it isn't a story any more, it's a bad joke. So I'm going to end this narrative like Gazza's narrative has ended, abruptly, unsatisfactorily.

PAUL BAILEY

Joe Orton

25 June 1994

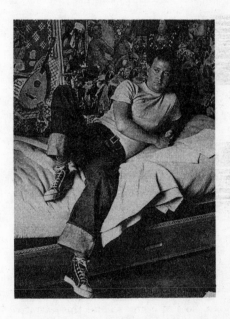

The novelist Paul Bailey celebrates the heroic unrespectability of the playwright Joe Orton, who would have relished the opportunities for satire in today's Britain

'Undoubtedly Jean Genet is the most perfect example of an unconscious humorist at work since Marie Corelli,' Joe Orton wrote in his diary in January 1967, after reading *Querelle of Brest*. He found parts of the novel 'irresistibly funny', noting that 'a combination of elegance and crudity is always ridiculous'. It was his intention to satirise Genet in a play to be called *Where Love Lies Bleeding*, in which the Romantic notion of the beautiful young murderer would be employed to comic effect. Orton himself was murdered later that year by Kenneth Halliwell, his companion and one-time mentor. Halliwell was neither young nor beautiful, and had become envious to the point of insanity of his protégé's success. He will be remembered for ever as the man who hammered to death a potentially great dramatist.

Joe Orton was not a believer in heroes or heroism, although he did acknowledge certain masters – Congreve, Sheridan, Wilde and Ronald Firbank. Many people (his detractors, usually) associate him with the Sixties, but his talent refuses to be confined to a mere decade. *What the Butler Saw*, which will guarantee his lasting reputation, is not a period piece – Dr Prentice's private clinic, like Algernon Moncrieff's rooms or Lady Wishfort's house, is the setting for ageless comedy. When the deranged Dr Rance says, 'I wish more scientists would keep their ideas to themselves,' and Mrs Prentice, catching a glimpse of the dress her husband is trying to hide from her, asks, 'Have you taken up transvestism?' and adds, 'I'd no idea our marriage teetered on the edge of fashion,' Orton is paying homage to the select writers who influenced him and yet writing in his own voice as well.

It isn't an entirely literary voice, however, thanks to Orton's ear for the contortions, dislocations and inventiveness of everyday speech. He enjoyed listening to Hilda and Ernest Corden, his neighbours in Islington, almost as much as reading *The School for Scandal* or *Cardinal Pirelli*. 'I've been given top-class penicillin,' Hilda told him when he visited her in hospital, and Ernest remarked of a mutual acquaintance, 'She's got a new carpet to think of. And as we all know, she's a most houseproud woman.' There were other philosophers and monologists who entertained him, overheard on bus journeys or encountered in the public lavatories, or 'cottages', he frequented. He occasionally gives the impression that his pleasure in the company of his fellow-cottagers was not restricted to sex. He was thrilled by their pattern, too, and recorded it in the diary Halliwell read with such assiduity, with such increasing distress.

Orton insisted that he was essentially a realist, and wanted actors to think of the events in his plays 'in terms of reality'. In a television production of *What the Butler Saw*, Dinsdale Landen, Timothy West and Prunella Scales played the leading roles as if they were level-headed human beings, and the result was hilarious. West's sweetly reasonable Dr Rance was a wonderful impersonation of a lunatic unaware of his lunacy, and that unawareness is what makes him funny.

There are playwrights who explore the infinite richness and diversity of life, but Orton did not live to be one of them. Perhaps he never would have been, since his devilish gift for cutting men and women down to size, for showing them at their most absurd, was still in the process of reaching full expression when he died. He seemed to be happy with subjects like sex and death, and with characters who represent the status quo – policemen, lawyers, doctors. He shared Ionesco's distrust of those in authority, and hated the face they offer to the world.

The various scandals in the Conservative Party that have diverted, or upset, the nation in the last few months are the very stuff of Orton's art. The unimaginable death of Stephen Milligan was well inside the bounds of his imagination, which delighted in the sometimes macabre demands of the libido. What angry relish the Back to Basics campaign would have afforded him, and how he would have chortled had he heard the seasoned adulterer who declared on radio, the week before Parliament met to debate lowering the age of consent for homosexuals, that 'homosexual behaviour is an abhorrence'. The England he was dispatched from in 1967 – the year the Wolfenden recommendations became law – has begun to parody itself in ways that might be properly deemed Ortonesque.

'Quite frankly, if you bed people that I call "below-stairs class" they go to the papers, don't they?' Jane Clark's famous line could have been put in the mouth of one of Orton's outraged ladies. Orton came from the 'below-stairs class', in common with several English geniuses. His plays give a view from below of the upstarts above, though the word 'vision' is probably more appropriate. I often wonder if the society he poked fun at would have exerted its terrible revenge on him had he lived – with the bestowal of a knighthood, for instance. 'Arise, Sir John Kingsley Orton' – no, no, not *him*; not that far-from-plain Joe; not the bright young rebel who first made me laugh when I was in my twenties, and continues to do so thirty years on. His heroic unrespectability remains intact for me, a source of continuing delight.

BERYL BAINBRIDGE

◇

Rasputin

10 September 1988

*The novelist finds herself drawn to the
'mad, bad monk', convinced that his
attitudes to life and politics deserve more
credit than they receive*

When Ben Hecht arrived in Hollywood to write scripts, it was pointed out to him that, although in a novel the hero could behave like a cad to numerous girls and yet marry a virgin, it was not the same on the screen.

In a film the hero, as well as the heroine, had to be a virgin. If he wasn't, then he was a villain. As such he could be as caddish as he liked and have as much fun as he wanted, cheating and stealing, getting rich and whipping the servants, just so long as he was shot in the end. When he fell with a bullet in his forehead, it was advisable that he clutch at the Gobelin tapestry on the library wall and bring it down over his head like a symbolic shroud.

It is not surprising that my generation, brought up on the movies in a less permissive age, would have had more time for villains than heroes. In fact the villains were our heroes. We could project on to the villain all our fear of foreigners, of authority – and also our secret desire for wealth, skulduggery and illicit sex.

Sometimes at the end of the picture the villain reformed, but it was more credible if he was shot. None of us could believe that a chap leading such an enviable – such a heroic – life would ever give it up voluntarily.

For a long time the hero-villains I most admired were all drawn from the cinema, until, through an elderly couple who lived in our village and who were members of the Communist Party, I learned about the Russian Revolution. I was shown photographs of all the prominent Bolsheviks, Litvinov, young Molotov, Dzerzhinski. For weeks I had a picture of Commissar Zinoviev pinned to my bedroom wall – he bore a striking resemblance to Ken Dodd – but I took him down as soon as I discovered Rasputin, that 'mad, bad monk' condemned by history as being the most powerful and wicked man in pre-revolutionary Russia.

He came to St Petersburg from Siberia, and in 1905, hearing of his powers as a healer, the Empress Alexandra sent for him to doctor her son, the haemophiliac Tsarevitch, who was bleeding to death from a fall.

Having successfully treated the child, Rasputin became an intimate of the royal family, although it was not until 1911 that he exerted any political influence.

In the beginning I suspect he was a true friend to Alexandra, a woman who was already unpopular because she considered court life superficial and preferred to spend her time with her husband. She was also prudish, religious, and naïve enough to want to understand the soul of the 'ordinary Russian'. That she should think the extraordinary Rasputin fitted into this category doesn't say much for her powers of perception, but then, he had saved her little boy.

It's true too that, like all villains, Rasputin has had his faults listed at the expense of his virtues, of which he must have had some, for why else would a refined and chaste woman seek the company of a licentious peasant who by all accounts had lice in his beard, dirt under his fingernails and atrocious table manners? It is said that he foresaw the disastrous results the First World War would have for the Romanovs and, though it was treason to do so, he constantly urged an end to hostilities.

The claim that he had supernatural powers could be dismissed were it not for the manner of his death, which was excessively prolonged and distressed its perpetrators almost as much as its victim.

On the night of 17 December 1916 Prince Yusupov invited

Rasputin to a concert. When it was over they went upstairs to drink champagne, followed by coffee into which the prince and his fellow-conspirators had put enough arsenic to kill everyone in the room.

Rasputin drank, smacked his lips and said he was going downstairs to listen to more music. He stayed there for an hour, apparently in the best of health, and, alarmed that he might soon leave the house, someone ran downstairs and shot him three times. Rasputin, still on his feet, swore loudly and said he would tell the Tsarina all about it in the morning.

Apart from a heavy sweat which dripped from his brow he seemed unharmed. It was then that a servant stabbed him through the back and he fell down. He would have got up again if they hadn't tied his hands and feet and bundled him into a car driven to the banks of the Neva River. Finding a hole in the ice, they pushed him in, and still he tried to get out. Then they held his head under and at last he died.

It has been written that he was one of the evillest men who ever lived. I prefer to think of him as a breath of rank air, so to speak, who blew away the cobwebs of the Imperial Palace and strode through the marble corridors in his cossack boots, ordering champagne by the bucket and generally being the life and soul of the party.

When you think who came after, he was, after all, quite a small villain.

CLIVE BARKER

◇

Edgar Allan Poe

30 November 1991

*The fantasy writer on his hero, a man
obsessed with death and depravity*

Heroes are a dangerous breed. Idolise them with too much passion and sooner or later they'll disappoint you. Unless, of course, you choose a hero whose life and work announces his frailties from the outset, allowing you to mould his image from the clay of which his feet are made.

Edgar Allan Poe is such a hero. One of the first books of *fantastique* fiction I purchased was Poe's *Tales of Mystery and Imagination*, in a paperback edition with a lurid cover. It cost, if memory serves, 2s 6d. I was ten or so and this seemed a fortune. But then treasure houses are seldom cheap.

There had always been books in my life, but until that edition of Poe I'd had to scour them for hints of the dark, taboo material I had an appetite for. Now, at last – here in my hands – was a book whose entire subject was death, obsession and depravity. My interest in the darker side of the fictions I'd read had never been smiled upon by my parents, which only perfected the pleasure by making it forbidden.

Looking back, I'm certain a good deal of the book must have been virtually incomprehensible to me. Poe is a difficult anchor for a young reader – his style often turgid, his language elaborate – and had it not been that there were drops of tainted liquor to be squeezed from this troublesome prose I might well have given up on it. But I revelled in the perversities he paraded: the discovery of the corpses in 'The Murders in the Rue Morgue', the return of Madeline in 'The Fall of the House of Usher', the unmasking of the Red Death. If the sexual sub-text of much of his fiction passed me by, much else did not.

I don't suppose the concept of decadence was something I was much aware of at the age of ten (maybe puberty brings that along), but I was, I'm sure, in love with the splendour of Poe's decaying systems, so much more entrancing than the banalities of a middle-class upbringing in Sixties Liverpool. I knew when reading him that I was in the company of a fellow-spirit.

Later, much later, I was to learn what a sad, sick, self-deceiving and destructive spirit he was. There are few facts about Poe's biography over which a cloud doesn't hang. Born in Boston, Massachusetts, in 1809, he was orphaned before he was three, and was later disowned by his foster-father, who viewed him as an irresponsible waster. In 1831 he was court-martialled and dishonourably discharged from West Point, where he was a cadet, for intentional neglect of his duties. In later life, though his stories and his criticism drew admiration and a measure of fame, his financial situation was always precarious, and on several occasions became desperate. His marriage in 1836 to his thirteen-year-old cousin Virginia was doomed (she died of tuberculosis). He was dead at forty, his frail constitution undone by the demands of grief and overwork.

He left a world behind him, however, wrought out of the very sicknesses and destructive impulses that would end his life so prematurely. A world circling on its own obsessions, devouring itself with frustration: fetid and rotting and wholly unique.

To read Poe is to step on to another planet. There is no landscape like it. And no story more perfectly embodies his genius than the half-dozen or so pages of 'The Masque of the Red Death'. In a world as determinedly abstract as anything in Shakespeare, a group of nobles gathers at Prince Prospero's palace to pleasure out a plague that is killing the world beyond the walls. But the Red Death comes visiting and claims the celebrants. It is a simple tale which Poe raises to fine art.

There's nothing in the narrative which relates to my personal experience, either then or now. The story confounds any assumption that for dark fantasy to achieve its intended *frisson* it must offer characters and settings the reader can readily identify with. Unlike much current work in the field, which offers the simple and simplistic vision of a contemporary status quo invaded by – and usually overcoming – some alien force, Poe offers the clarity of a fable told in the baroque, hallucinatory style of an opium poet. Not for him the easy chill of suburbia possessed: the lawnmower speaking in tongues, and the youngest returning from the cemetery with his head on backwards. Poe was interested in making myths, and he originated forms by which countless writers have shaped their work. The ground rules for the fictions of obsession, of detection, even, arguably, areas of science fiction, were laid out in his brief, intense tales.

But rules are only useful if the game is worth playing, and Poe proved to me early in my imaginative life the power of fictions that are unabashedly committed to the business of taboo. He taught me that if the vision was strong enough it didn't matter if the story occurred yesterday on your own street corner or on some dateless day in an unnamed place. After Poe, the thrust of *fantastique* fiction would never for me be a matter of conventional folks setting their Christian values against some fretful, haunted darkness, but a celebration, however perverse, of that darkness; a call to enter a territory where no image or act is so damnable it cannot be explored, turned over in the mind's eye, kissed and courted; finally – why whisper it? – *embraced*.

RONAN BENNETT

◇

Patrice Lumumba

7 August 1993

*The novelist on his hero, the idealistic
Congolese leader*

It has become fashionable, as South Africa inches painfully towards majority rule, for cynics to malign the fallen heroes of the first generation of African nationalist leaders, those whose programmes for independence were populist, socialist and pan-African. The warning runs: South Africans are better off now than they will be after the blacks come to power. Look at Kenya, Ghana, Zambia. Just look at Zaire.

That Zaire is now a hell-hole is no fault of Patrice Lumumba, the man reviled as a 'barbarian' from the time, in the mid-Fifties, when he surfaced as a nationalist leader in what was then the Belgian Congo. In the view of a British journalist, Lumumba 'personified the emergent Africa in politics . . . a have-not of obscure parentage, with a smouldering grudge against the white man'.

Lumumba's crime was his refusal to go along with the Belgians' manipulative plans for post-independence Congo. On Independence Day, 30 June 1960, as the country's first elected prime minister, he told King Baudouin of the Belgians: 'Carve this date upon your hearts . . . We have submitted morning, noon and night to jeers, insults and blows . . . We are your monkeys no more.'

It was vintage Lumumba. Opponents described his speech as inflammatory and resentful, but it appeals to me for its forthright expression of contempt for the colonists. I admire fixedness of political purpose, and Lumumba is a reminder that there was once a time when this quality was possessed in greater quantity by the Left than by the Right. He knew that to be moderate when your opponents are ruthless is to win plaudits for maturity but otherwise to surrender the interests of your constituency.

Lumumba remained until his death the uncompromising

leader of his country's poor and disenfranchised. He strove to thwart the Belgians, who went through the motions of handing over power in the full and arrogant expectation that 'monkeys' would continue to do their bidding.

Lumumba's idealism, however, led him to make a critical mistake. Just a few months after his election, the Belgians sabotaged his government by aiding Moise Tshombe's secessionist movement in the mineral-rich province of Katanga. Lumumba appealed to the newly elected Eisenhower administration, and later to Kennedy. But the Americans had already marked him down as Africa's Castro. The CIA station chief in Léopoldville cabled Washington: 'Congo experience classic Communist takeover ... Whether or not Lumumba actually Commie or just playing Commie game to assist his solidifying power, anti-West forces rapidly increasing power.'

Lumumba turned to the Soviet Union, which supplied non-military aid, but it was on the United Nations that he pinned his hopes. He took the UN's anti-colonial rhetoric at face value. It was to be his undoing, for he failed to appreciate that a convergence of Cold War and colonial interests meant the UN's aim in Africa was to safeguard the West's influence. Instead of assisting Lumumba's democratically elected government, UN 'peace-keepers' deposed him. He was taken prisoner by Tshombe's CIA-backed forces and murdered in January 1961.

Lumumba possessed all the qualities of the popular revolutionary leader: relentless energy, powerful oratory, identification with the poor. He had advanced ideas on the position of women, condemned racism, and fought against the tribalism exploited by the colonists and their stooges. He had a generosity of spirit and an easy intimacy. He also had a reckless, outgoing quality – an attractive contrast with the caution of most politicians but a serious flaw in a leader, and one that takes Lumumba into the realm of the tragic hero. The political animal in me wants to rebuke Lumumba for allowing his flaws to lead him into disaster; the writer in me is drawn to heroic failure.

The photographs of Lumumba in captivity show him surrounded by soldiers, hands tied behind his back, face swollen from beatings. I've studied the pictures, looked for the hero's defiance in the face of death – and it isn't there. Instead there is trepidation. This doesn't lower Lumumba in my estimation. He was thirty-five years old, and did not want to die – which is fair enough. For me, it is sufficient that the man lived a hero.

MICHAEL BRACEWELL

Billy Fury

29 August 1992

*The novelist Michael Bracewell on his
idea of a rock 'n' roll idol*

If one manages to meet one's hero, it's usually a big mistake: tongue-tied and cowed in the presence of greatness, one reveals the worst possible version of oneself, and the memory of such a humiliation is apt to linger. The true dialogue which exists between a fan and a hero is too complicated, and too intense, to permit a close encounter.

For this reason – I have come to believe – it is better to have a dead hero. When disenchanting details about dead heroes come to light (and we all, deep down, resent new biographies of our heroes) one can simply deny them, and question their source. In fact, the less one knows about one's hero the better; as with many forms of love, love for a hero thrives upon distance and obscurity. In keeping with this propensity for romantic vagueness, my heroes have changed like the shades of white in which my room has been painted: white with a hint of rose (Keats), white with a hint of leaf green (Wilde), white with a hint of white (Warhol).

Heroes arrive unexpectedly, like interesting television programmes or letters from abroad. This, at least, has been my experience of them, and my current hero was no exception. Four months ago, when I was thirty-three and a half, I happened upon a poorly attended Billy Fury convention in Wigan. I was between heroes at the time. My attention was caught as much by the corroding civic grandeur of the hall in which it was held as it was by the strains of 'Fury's Tune' echoing within. Beyond the hall, in the middle distance, I could see an advertisement painted on the wall of the factory; it said: UNCLE JOE'S MINT BALLS KEEP YOU ALL AGLOW. Then the music changed and 'A Thousand Stars', waltz-like and soaring, filled the air. As Proust contemplated the hawthorn bush at Reveillon and subsequently sought to recapture the sensation of its initial impact, so I, buffeted by Billy and mesmerised by MINT BALLS, stood rooted to the pavement in Wigan, recognising some sudden surge of beauty. A moment of mysterious harmony had taken place, as befitted the entrance of a hero: Billy Fury, out of a Wigan shrine, seemed to be singing to me personally. Music, mood and meaning had spontaneously combined to make all things, particularly in that neck of the North West, seem precious. Acknowledging Billy to be the presiding genius over this rare moment of insight, I paid my £1.20 (plus membership fee) and entered his convention.

It doesn't really matter that Billy Fury was born Ron Wyncherley, in Liverpool, in 1941. It only matters slightly that he talked his way, aged seventeen, through the stage door of Birkenhead's Essoldo Theatre and won the heart of impresario Larry Parnes with a quick demonstration of his rock 'n' roll crooning. But it does matter, greatly, that Billy Fury looked like a teenage pop idol ought to look: golden quiff, leopard-print shirt, lamé suit, unimaginatively handsome and cheerfully rebellious. Add to this the fact that, tragically, he had a heart condition, and all you need is a pedestal to place him on and a pillow under which to keep his photograph. Billy Fury is what you'd find in the Yellow Pages under 'Heroes'.

I imagine that, in 1961, when Billy recorded 'Would You Stand by Me?', an army of fans whispered *Yes*. For the boys, Billy Fury must have served as an enviable role model for some unobtainable genius for self-expression; for the girls (and photographs of the girls survive: an ocean of waved autograph books and lumpy hairdos crashing against Billy's chest), he must have seemed simply unobtainable, and thus the perfect dream lover. Billy's big hit 'Halfway to Paradise' is the perfect theme for the relationship between hero and fan – never quite getting there, but savouring an ecstatic frustration.

In Wigan, surrounded by couples from the *Z Cars* generation and a few defensive Teds, I also realised why, after years of guilt and feigned expressions of interest, I cannot listen to jazz without falling into a deep, immediate sleep. In comparison to rock 'n' roll, and the crooned rock 'n' roll ballad, jazz seems like a pallid mess. This is probably unfair, but I suddenly felt as though Fury had liberated me from a responsibility to appreciate pre-pop music. Thus, in one hour and twenty minutes, Billy Fury had become my new hero for three reasons: he sounded brilliant, his photograph would look ideal in a gold frame on a white wall, and he had stopped me from worrying about jazz. Clutching three LPs and a postcard, I wondered at how the best music comes from the North: The Fall, the Pet Shop Boys, Morrissey and now Billy Fury. It must be something they put in the mint balls.

Billy died, aged forty-one, in 1983. His last years were not successful. It is a sad fact that such a dismal, protracted twilight to a life often serves to seal glamour. It is unlikely, at this point in time, that Billy Fury will suddenly become fashionable. Canvassing my friends, I am partially relieved to discover that I alone wish to dust Billy's bust in the rock 'n' roll hall of fame. But I knew in Wigan, as I know now, that Billy Fury was that rarest of stars: a man with a voice like velvet or a motorcycle roar; dramatic, glamorous, and English. God bless Wigan, home of the unexpected.

CRAIG BROWN

◇

Noele Gordon

20 November 1993

*The humorist and columnist has identified
a spooky precursor to Baroness Thatcher
behind the desk at Crossroads Motel*

Watching Lady Thatcher's four-part series on television, I kept thinking to myself: Hmmmm, you remind me of someone. But who? The neat, tough suits; the stiff, bouncy hair; the complete self-assurance; the somewhat over-dramatic, almost camp, facial expressions; all those crises, and all that coping. Then it struck me: it's Noele Gordon.

Of course, Noele Gordon was no stranger to Downing Street herself. In 1975 – the year of Margaret Thatcher's succession to the leadership of the Conservative Party – Harold Wilson's wife, Mary, generally a shrinking violet when it came to public endorsements, wrote the foreword, headed '10 Downing Street, Whitehall', for Noele Gordon's seminal autobiography, *My Life at Crossroads*. It was only brief, but it hit the nail on the head. 'I am sure many women see Noele Gordon in the character of Meg Richardson as the type of woman they themselves would like to be – understanding, sensible, able to cope with any situation,' she wrote. 'Also, women like to look at Meg's clothes – she is always well-dressed and groomed!'

Did those few, well-chosen words have any influence on the then Leader of the Opposition? We shall probably never know – Gordon, Noele, is nowhere to be found in the index of *The Downing Street Years* – but the similarities between Noele Gordon's creation, Meg Richardson, and Margaret Thatcher are so plentiful as to be uncanny.

Apart from looking, sounding and dressing the same, both Meg and Margaret had to cope as female bosses in a man's world – in Margaret's case, the cut-throat world of politics, in Meg's, the cut-throat world of Birmingham catering. Both had two children, a boy (Mark/Sandy) and a girl (Carol/Jilly) who, though essentially homebound, were forever getting into scrapes and hanging out with the wrong types. Both Meg and Margaret were married to millionaire businessmen (Denis/ Hugh) who, though always on hand with sound advice, were fully prepared to take a back seat. Both Meg and Margaret exhibited a penchant for debonair types in slinky suits as their right-hand man (Cecil Parkinson/David Hunter) and both Cecil and David were to experience grave problems in their own marriages, though, to my almost certain knowledge, Cecil's wife never wounded him with a shotgun, as David's found herself doing. Margaret was voted Prime Minister on three consecutive occasions, while Meg won the *TV Times* award for 'Most Compulsive Character' on no less than eight consecutive occasions.

And, of course, both Meg and Margaret were to come to sticky ends after all that time at the top. After seventeen years playing the proprietor of Crossroads Motel, Noele Gordon was ousted on 22 June 1981. After fifteen years playing the leader of the Conservative Party, Margaret Thatcher was ousted on 22 November 1990. Both made last-ditch attempts to hang on to power (NOELE'S DESPERATE PLEA 'SAVE ME, LEW!' – *Sunday Mirror* headline, 28 June 1981) but to no avail. Both Margaret and Meg were pictured departing in tears ('I am stunned with sorrow' – Noele Gordon, 30 June 1981), though their unhappiness was not shared by one and all. Jack Straw called Margaret 'this evil woman', while the *Daily Star* ran a competition ('How would you get rid of her? Shoot her? Blow her up?') to signal Meg's demise, the £25 prize eventually going to the reader who suggested she should be beaten to death with a frying-pan. Finally, both women were replaced by somewhat faceless men and both shows petered to a close. Intimates suggested that neither woman ever quite recovered from the shock of rejection, retreating behind a mask of bravado, appearing in other shows, but never finding a role of the same stature.

But Noele Gordon's spooky, Nostradamus-like artistic pre-science – let us never forget that her career pre-dated Margaret Thatcher's by a good ten years – is not the only reason I have chosen her as my heroine. Hers was the most reassuring television presence of any. Like David Frost, only more so, she possessed the great gift of complete unflappability. Her professional manner was professional, yet warm ('Hello, Cross-roads Motel. Can I help you?'), and even in the midst of personal crisis – one week a blackmail threat, the next a psychopathic killer on the loose – she would have an encouraging word for one and all ('Why don't you put that gun away, dear? I'm sure we can sort this out in a more civilised manner. Sherry?').

People watch television to relax, and Noele Gordon was tremendously relaxing. When Noele – or was it Meg? – was on screen, you knew you were in safe hands, you knew that sets could wobble, that telephones could start ringing long after they had been answered, that posses of ruthless kidnappers, vengeful wives and mysterious lords could make a beeline for the chalets, or that – my personal favourite of all the story lines – Amy Turtle could be (falsely) exposed as the Russian spy Amelia Turtulovski, but for as long as Meg – or was it Noele? – was around, nothing could ever go really wrong: she might sigh, she might raise a sceptical eyebrow, she might even take comfort from a single schooner of medium sherry, but, my God, she would cope.

GORDON BURN

◆

Tom Pickard

25 January 1992

*The writer Gordon Burn celebrates
the wild Tyneside poet Tom Pickard,
who taught him there was more to
literature than set texts*

'You can't write, you're only half-literate, you haven't even GCE O levels, your poetry consists of emotional distress signals, illiterate name-droppings, improper spelling of proper nouns and intellectual cloud bursts, you've been seen to piss on floors in pubs, which you're never out of except at closing time. You spend the time between opening hours picking crab lice from your pubic hair and getting into debt. You steal and smoke dope tabs, have intercourse with anyone who is willing to open their legs for you. When you do get poetry readings you become so pissed you fall offstage and sometimes have to be thrown off because of your irreverent behaviour towards the audience, most of whom come from respectable homes . . .'

This account of a typical browbeating from the people he depended on for hand-outs in the Sixties (the National Assistance Board and North-East Arts) comes from Tom Pickard's heavily autobiographical novel *Guttersnipe*, a book which occupies territory somewhere between early Lawrence and Hubert Selby Jnr's *Last Exit to Brooklyn*.

Guttersnipe was published in America in 1970 by City Lights Books in San Francisco, home of the Beats, and imported into Britain with a testimonial from City Lights' founder, Lawrence Ferlinghetti: 'Tom Pickard . . . writes in a rough voice, in the Newcastle dialect, and he came to Oxford with us and he read a poem on a gangbang in this Newcastle dialect – he really woke things up with this big rough voice.'

I was sixteen in 1964. Pickard was only two years older, and from a virtually identical background (his father shovelled coal in the railway yards in Gateshead; mine worked in a factory on the Tyne). But whereas I was a conventional product of the system, a standard roll-on, roll-off grammar-school achiever, he was already married to a beautiful older woman,

Connie (a name throbbing with *Chatterley* connotations at that time), and four years into what he referred to as 'my working life on the dole'. His insistence on registering himself as 'poet' – 'I didn't want to be an engine-cleaner. Not for a lifetime. I didn't want to be anything for a lifetime,' he wrote in *Guttersnipe* – drove the paper-pushers at the Youth Employment Bureau up the wall.

At the age of eighteen, Pickard had got hold of Morden Tower, a medieval turret he rented on the old town walls by the bus station, and launched the series of readings and 'happenings' which were the first sign to me that writing could be something more than a set text to be slogged through with dutiful encirclings and underlinings and comments of 'v. imp' and 'signif' in the margins.

Pickard's first task when he took over Morden Tower was to track down Basil Bunting in Wylam, outside Newcastle, and convince him that there was a new young audience for his poetry; Bunting had written nothing since *The Spoils* in 1951, and it's probably fair to say there would have been none of the hard-won late poems without Pickard's friendly bullying.

Basil Bunting was the first writer I ever saw reading his work – an old man in pebble glasses and a lumpy winter suit, a living link (I now know) with Ford Madox Ford, Hemingway, Yeats, Eliot, Pound and Zukofsky. Although he was virtually unknown in his own country, Bunting had a considerable reputation among younger American poets as an important figure in the Modernist movement. And it was this, in the beginning, that drew Ginsberg, Creeley, Hollo, Corso, Ferlinghetti and others to the North East.

For the first few years, Morden Tower didn't have electricity. Writers read by gaslight with the bearded meditators and 'holy creeps', the nervous grammar-school boys and pioneer 'cosmonauts of inner space' sprawled on the cold stone floor in front of them. People relieved themselves in the Northumberland Arms at the head of the alley, or flooded the fat black cobbles.

I have a clear memory of Allen Ginsberg standing on the ramparts alongside Morden Tower, pissing in a steaming arc twenty feet over my head. At his shoulder, wearing a muffler and a plastic-shouldered donkey-jacket, his long hair strobing in the back-light, Tom Pickard glugged on another bottle of the drink known as 'lunatic juice' or 'o cosmic one' – Newcastle Brown Ale. Clamped between the fingers of his free hand, more than likely, was a 'dope tab' of best Pakistani black.

The intoxication that Pickard showed in the presence of his heroes was an amplification of the excitement he got from their work. The spirit of Morden Tower was headily unbookish, although it was filled floor-to-ceiling with books – Bunting, the Beats, Marcuse, Reich, Ouspensky, *The Ginger Man*, *The Naked Lunch*, *Candy*, *Lolita* – in the dangerous green covers of the Olympia Press.

The place Tom Pickard made offered an alternative to official culture, to the mystique and snobbery associated with the arts. 'It's not a fuckin' morgue yi na,' Pickard's automatic bellowed reaction to being told to keep his voice down in the civic citadels of culture, could have been its motto. It was the Scottish writer Alexander Trocchi's notion of 'a cultural jam-session', a 'spontaneous university' made flesh.

JOHN BURNINGHAM

◇

A. S. Neill

7 November 1992

*John Burningham, a writer and illustrator
of children's books, remembers his hero,
the headmaster who abolished authority at
his school, Summerhill*

I like tangos. For years I didn't know why, but now I wonder if it has anything to do with the fact that Alexander Sutherland Neill, head of Summerhill, liked tangos.

In my day (1948–1952) it was known as the Do As You Please School. Now it is known as the school where they chop rabbits' heads off, as seen on TV. I cannot remember my first day there, but I do remember that it was somehow different and this had something to do with Neill.

Neill ('Neill, Neill, orange peel,' we used to chant) was quite a shy man. He was large and stooping with big ears with long lobes which he would wiggle between thumb and finger when in conversation and he wore boots like Gertrude Jekyll's, which were made to his specifications for 'extra-wide Scottish feet'. He was kind and gentle with a keen sense of value for money. I vividly remember going on an outing with him to buy a bolt for the door of my room. We had a choice – the 3d or the 3½d. He firmly chose the former.

I learned subsequently that he had endured the rigours of the Scottish schooling system, including corporal punishment by the tawse. My Oxford dictionary tells me now that this is 'an instrument of family or school discipline used in Scottish and some English schools, consisting of a leather strap or thong, divided at the end into narrow strips'.

In a letter home one of the boys wrote 'there's a man here called Neill', and that seemed to sum up my initial impression of him very well. He was a presence rather than a dominating figurehead – part of the school in every sense, and thinking about it now I realise that Mr Gumpy, a central character in two of my books, is really the unconscious expression of my memories of Neill.

For a few terms at Summerhill I lived in one of three

railway carriages, covered by a tin roof. It housed about twelve to fourteen boys and was heated by a coke-fuelled Tortoise stove. The carriages were quite some way down a long track from the main school building and I remember, on one occasion, being chased down the path by a ferocious goose as I returned from collecting some coke for the stove. Food was rationed and there never seemed quite enough. The food store was the Fort Knox of Summerhill and we dreamed of its contents.

I think it was Michael Proudlock (forgive me, Mr Proudlock, if you have been wrongly accused) who initially stole the Fort Knox key, but somehow Toby Jelinek and I (now it can be told) got hold of it. For what seemed like weeks we revelled in an orgy of late-night consumption of tinned fruit and Carnation milk. I used to throw the empties out of the railway-carriage window into the bushes behind. It reached a point where it was hard to throw a can out without hitting another one.

But the day of reckoning had to come. I was visiting Neill's house for reasons I now forget. I found him in his sitting room, buried behind a newspaper and only his large boots were visible.

'Some bugger has got the key to the store room, Brum,' he said from behind the paper. 'You wouldn't happen to know who that is would you?' I left immediately and returned, minutes later, with the key. A hand emerged from the side of the paper and took it. 'Thank you very much,' said Neill and continued to read. I departed.

This experience was just one of many Summerhill escapades, but it has stayed with me. In any other school I would probably have been beaten and/or expelled. If I had been older, I would probably have been detained at Her Majesty's Pleasure. Whatever, Neill gave me freedom and a chance to develop my own framework of belief. Certainly, it was my last sortie into organised crime and nowadays I find it hard to even throw a matchstick out of a car window.

Of course, my Summerhill education was inadequate – isn't every type of education inadequate in some way? Why didn't someone make me play a musical instrument or put a tennis racquet in my hand? I was, however, able to spend a great deal of time in the art room, and for this I am eternally grateful.

I've not been back for years. I don't keep up with old schoolfriends. I have not sent my children there, perhaps because I want to keep it separate from what has happened since. But I do know that one of my most enduring memories is that of the Saturday school dance, when the jazz 78s (the in-thing then) had to stop for one of Neill's tangos, and a loud groan would go up as the large boots and long ears would glide across the well-worn floor accompanied by an obliging young lady.

As John Patten thunders about our apparent 'loss of fear in the eternal consequences of goodness and badness' and the 'lack of morality and rise of criminality' in the young, I am reminded of Neill's words: 'How can happiness be bestowed? My own answer is abolish authority. Let the child be himself. Don't push him around. Don't teach him. Don't lecture him ... It may not be your answer. But if you reject my answer, it is incumbent on you to find a better one.'

They are both radical views, but I wonder whose ideas will stand the test of time. I have a sneaking suspicion that they could be those of Alexander Sutherland Neill.

JOHN BYRNE

◇

René Magritte

5 November 1988

The author of the television series
Tutti Frutti *remembers the impact of*
the Surrealist in the bowler hat

In 1925 the poet Marcel Lecomte showed René Magritte a reproduction of Giorgio de Chirico's 'The Song of Love', a painting from 1914 that shows an antique mask, a surgeon's glove and a green ball juxtaposed with an Italian townscape of deep afternoon shadows, with a train passing just behind the wall on which the mask and the glove are mounted. The three (ostensibly) unrelated objects assume a monstrous presence, quite out of scale with their surroundings. So moved was the Belgian artist that 'almost overnight' he became a Surrealist. Magritte was twenty-seven.

In 1958 in a room at the Tate I came face to face with my first Magritte. 'Time Transfixed' was painted in 1939 and shows a railway engine coming out of an otherwise perfectly ordinary boarded-up fireplace in an empty sitting room. The clock on the mantelpiece shows the time as coming up to a quarter to one. Two candlesticks flank the clock. The large mirror above the fireplace reflects the back of the clock and one of the candlesticks, nothing else. When I look at the painting now I am struck by its tranquillity, its perfect reasonableness. Thirty-one years ago I found it deeply disturbing. It haunted me for years. I hated it.

Charlie and I were first-year students down in London from Glasgow School of Art. It was his bright idea to spend our days trudging round the galleries. I mean every gallery. We would set out from Archway, where we were lodging with my Uncle Hughie and his wife Gladys, head for the tube with a copy of *Arts Review* and systematically 'do' the exhibitions listed.

It was a very hot summer. I remember my gums started to bleed in Cork Street on this particular day. Charlie expressed a burning desire to visit the Dalis on loan from Chicago to

Millbank. I held the bloody rag to my mouth and told him I'd had quite enough Surrealism for one afternoon, thank you. But he was most persistent. I capitulated. The Dalis were OK. A bit slippery, but OK.

What got me in that loan exhibition was this painting of the train. Neither of us was rightly sure if 'René Magritte' was a man or a woman. I can't say if Charlie was as upset by the painting as I was.

The technique was deadpan. Only it wasn't a funny picture. Magritte's steam engine accompanied us all the way back on the Underground to north London. I couldn't get it out of my head.

That night, the dumb loco shunted back and forth in my dreams. It was almost ten years before it hit the buffers and the centime dropped. That it did eventually and I came to regard Magritte with joy is thanks in no small measure to George Melly and the film he made on the artist for the BBC in 1967.

I didn't become a Surrealist but I did become a fan. I got out my sketchbook and dashed off a letter to Belgium (I should've scribbled a note to dear George at the same time. Let me do that now. Dear Mr M, Thanks. Yrs sincerely, JB), never expecting it to get there.

Imagine my delight when a couple of weeks later I discovered a strange yellow envelope on the mat as I was setting off for work. There on the front were six funny pink stamps . . . in the top left-hand corner an address sticker: 97 Rue des Mimosas, Bruxelles III. Inside were seven postcards and a letter in Magritte's own hand. 'Cher Monsieur Byrne,' it began. But then it would, wouldn't it?

He went on to say how he too had worked in a design

49

studio, had painted in the evenings and on Sundays ... '*Il convient, je crois, à chacun de passer au travers de ces années d'épreuve, sans espoir et sans désespoirs. La vie m'est — actuellement — "plus facile", mais je sais qu'il n'y a rien de nécessaire à apprendre. Il est question du mystère dans ma peinture, c'est pour cette raison que je continue à peindre — je ne connais pas la raison qu'il y a de vivre et de mourir. (S'il y a une raison de vivre et de mourir dans un univers mystérieux.)*'

He apologised for the time it had taken him to reply to my letter. I wrote off thanking him for the reproductions. This time there was no response. I discovered much later that he'd died that summer.

It seems of little consequence, but one of the things I liked about Magritte was the fact that he didn't look like a painter. So, what does a painter look like, you ask? Well, having been brought up at my mother's knee with a portrait of the artist as a wild-eyed, one-eared messiah, living on pints of absinthe in the back room of some Parisian brothel and quite incapable of distinguishing between a wage packet and a wombat's udder, Magritte with his *chapeau melon* and little dog was like a breath of fresh air. Here was a true Secret Agent of Art. A man of our time ... of my time. Like Warhol after him, he'd actually soiled his hands, not in an art school, but in the real world.

He'd painted posters, illustrations. He'd drawn fur coats for catalogues, designed wallpapers. And still he's one of the great painters of the twentieth century. One of the little post-cards he sent me is entitled '*Le Tombeau des Lutteurs*'. It shows an enormous red rose crammed into an otherwise perfectly ordinary bedroom.

It's beautiful.

CRAIG CHARLES

<hr>

Bluto

18 December 1993

*Craig Charles, comedian, Scouser
and star of* Red Dwarf, *rehabilitates
Bluto, the misunderstood victim
of Popeye's mad rage*

Popeye and Bluto. Here we have, in microcosm, the perfect example of the downtrodden hero and the ruthless bully. I must confess to feeling a debt of gratitude to *The Independent Magazine* for allowing me this platform on which to air my views on what has been, if not a bee in my bonnet, then at least a wildebeest in my Lada since I was a mere Scouseling in the flush of youth.

As a seminal Scouseling, I was on the receiving end of an Olympic-standard clip round the ear for whacking Philip Browne over the head with a sock full of marbles. 'It's not big or clever to strike an unarmed person when you yourself are tooled up with a weighty sock full of marbles, young Mr Charles,' intoned the faceless figure of authority. 'But sir,' quoth I, 'just this morning I witnessed my hero Popeye turn into a jet fighter with twin machine guns and blast big old unarmed Bluto into oblivion.'

'Let me explain more clearly,' smiled the amiable pedagogue, as the marble-filled sock arched through the air, whistling a song about headaches. 'There, do you think that was fair?' he said when I came round. I had to admit that it had seemed a great deal fairer when it had been me in charge of the sock. So, I fell to thinking.

Herein is the kernel of my reasoning. How can we feel anything but abject sympathy for the poor, beleaguered Bluto when Popeye, clearly under the influence of a potent hallucinogen, converts his arms into massive steam hammers and bludgeons poor, unarmed Bluto into unconsciousness? Who can deny the blatant racism implicit in the act of a tattooed yob in a paramilitary uniform beating up someone of Mediterranean extraction for the simple reason that he just happens to be in the same cartoon? Wars have been started for less. Sad Bluto is clearly the product of a broken home and his laboured diction hints at someone for whom the phrase 'intellectually challenged' might well have been coined. When we bear in mind these factors, we can only admire the bravery of a man who daily faces physical and verbal assaults from a deranged bully and yet refuses to give in.

Let's face it, Popeye the sailor man is a complete 'weigh-anchor'. His bizarrely distorted musculature is obviously the result of an excessive intake of anabolic steroids. And what's he got in that pipe? What is this curious substance that turns him from an everyday tattooed dock rat into a ranting psycho-path with a voice like John Major on helium? He calls it 'spinach'. When a Rasta pops out to pick up some 'herb', we don't expect to find him perusing racks of oregano and thyme in the local Supersaver. Likewise, enthusiasts of 'grass' or 'weed' are rarely to be found skulking about the garden in unfashionable trousers and worn-out shoes. So, what is this 'spinach' that the evil Popeye is hooked on? It must be bloody strong. Only the most crazed junkie would manage to earn the name 'Popeye'. Think about it: POP EYE. It conjures up visions of a goggle-eyed lunatic with both lamps on full beam. A cross between the drug dealer from *Withnail and I* and a Rottweiler. Throw in a set of ridiculous inflatable forearms, a camp sailor suit and a squeaky voice and what have you got? I don't know, but I wouldn't want to meet it without an Uzi and a cattle prod handy.

But what of poor Bluto, riddled with neuroses and clearly self-conscious about his weight problem, which was almost certainly caused by too many pizzas in front of the television as he sat at home, alone and friendless, pining for his one true love, the faithless Olive Oyl? That outrageous, hyperactive, anorexic tart who is forever waving her legs at him in a lustful frenzy before giving him the elbow as soon as Popeye, her fellow-speed-freak, turns up with his stash. And what of the love-child, Sweepee. You don't have to be an expert in genetic fingerprinting to see that the child is Bluto's. What an agony of torment the poor man must be going through. To be denied even basic visiting rights while you watch the object of your love cavort with a dope-crazed maniac whose vocabulary consists of incoherent babbling punctuated by 'yuk yuk yuk'. I ask you: is this any kind of a father figure for a growing child? If we examine the classic *Popeye Out West*, the establishing shot is of 'Olive Oyl's Café and Music Hall' which, I feel, gives us a good indication of the kind of woman Ms Oyl is and the kind of environment she considers proper for the formative years of an impressionable child. It is also worth noting that in this very film the despicable Popeye initiates a chain of escalating violence by striking the first blow and later turns into a train, which any devotee of the Queensberry rules would consider a tad unfair.

The physical and psychological torment that the noble, upstanding Bluto bears so stoically serves as a beacon of hope for the human race. We should all spare a kind thought in this festive season for this poor, misunderstood man who hides his shyness behind a huge beard and conceals his love in a massive, broken heart.

LIZA CODY

◇

Klondyke Kate

25 July 1992

*Novelist Liza Cody on her heroine Klondyke
Kate, a British Ladies Wrestling Champion
who plays very dirty*

The first time I saw Klondyke Kate in person was one dark rainy night at the Bath Pavilion. The MC introduced her as 'the official British Ladies Wrestling Champion', but she didn't come out. The crowd howled. She was balking because the management had got her music wrong. Someone in the back row yelled, 'Play "Roll Out the Barrel". She'll come out to that.' Everyone laughed, but eventually she appeared. The first thing I heard her say was 'Shut yer mouth. Shut yer *dirty* mouth.' This was before she reached the ring. She snarled her way through an unruly mob of hissing, spitting people, already winding them up, already threatening and playing dirty. The Ladies Champion was *not* a lady.

Wrestling is basic entertainment, rude in the old sense of the word, and a wrestling crowd is not an opera crowd. The people who go to the fights are not there for subtlety or aesthetics. They want stories. They are a panto audience thirty years on, and they want to be part of the act. They need heroes and villains. In the ring, Klondyke Kate is a villain, but she is a heroine to me.

She breaks all the rules. She is fat and she shows it off in a black leotard, under bright lights, in front of hundreds of jeering, sneering men and women. Most overweight women hide. Klondyke Kate leans over the ropes and shouts, 'What are you looking at? Eh? Eh?'

She talks back. By no stretch of the imagination could she be called deferential. If you insult her, she insults you in return. 'My arse is prettier than your face,' a man screams. 'Come up and show us,' Kate screams back.

'Ignore them,' my mother used to say to me when I came home bleeding internally from some playground slight. 'Show them you're above it all.' I couldn't. I wasn't. I always made matters worse by fighting back. But like most little girls I wanted to be loved and approved of. So when I grew up I learned to control my temper. I taught myself to be nice. Most of the time. Women are supposed to look good, to behave well, to court love and approval.

Klondyke Kate doesn't. She glares across the ring at her little, perky opponent and shows no sympathy for her knee bandage. She will work mercilessly on that hurt knee later. She is not in the ring to show that women are the nurturing, caring sex. She is there to win by fair means or foul – preferably foul. A villain is supposed to play dirty, and Kate takes the job seriously.

One thing that Channel 4's coverage of sumo has taught us is that fat people can be athletic. They can be very fast and very strong. Klondyke Kate is a fast, strong wrestler. She need not bite, choke, pull hair, stomp or gouge. She could win fairly, if she wanted to. She does not because it is her job to be the villain, and she is forced to be the villain because she is big and does not look pretty in a leotard. She does not look like what our culture demands of a heroine. She is not large-eyed, long-legged, glossy-haired, neat or petite.

Not many women have enough courage to be unpopular. It goes against our conditioning. We try hard to be acceptable. We try to look acceptable. If we are fat, we diet. If we're hairy, we depilate. If we are not pretty, we compensate with make-up and humour. If we are angry or ambitious, we hide it as far as we can. Kate does none of this. I don't know if she would rather be the popular heroine. If she would, it doesn't show, and in any case nature didn't give her much choice. She makes the best of a bad job by becoming a beautiful villain.

So there she is in the middle of the ring, a barrel in black tights. She smashes, mashes and crushes her opponent. The game little thing, pretty in pink, fights back. Kate becomes quite evil. She cheats blatantly. The crowd goes berserk. 'Dirty slag!' they scream.

A little old man is so furious that he bounds out of his seat and runs down the aisle to the ringside. The bouncers are waiting for him, but he stops short. He is beside himself with rage and probably hasn't moved this fast for forty years.

'You . . .' he screams, 'you . . .' Spittle flies from his mouth glittering like diamonds in the spotlights. He cannot think of anything bad enough to say. Finally it comes out: 'You . . . you *bucket nut*!' he screeches.

'Come up here,' Kate sneers at the hysterical old man. 'We'll see who's got a bucket nut!' Kate's face – her bucket nut – says it all. It isn't a face to look at over the teacups.

Afterwards, when it was all over, I went to talk to Kate. She had been disqualified – there was no way her opponent could have won if she hadn't – and I was a little nervous. But the outrageous villain was calmly signing autographs at the back of the hall. She was watching the time, she said, because she had to get home to her little boy.

'What's your weak point?' I asked. 'As a fighter, I mean.'

'These,' she said, and she held out her hands. 'I keep breaking my fingers.' Her hands were tiny. 'I have to wear children's rings and gloves.'

Up there, behind the ropes, she had been so big and mean I'd never even noticed.

ROBIN COOK

◇

Esmond Romilly

8 January 1994

*The late Robin Cook, better known
as the author Derek Raymond, on his
rebellious hero Esmond Romilly, who died
tragically at the age of twenty-four*

Writer and public school *revolté* that I am, how can I resist naming Esmond Romilly in my small pantheon of heroes? You only have to look at his record. Born in 1917, a nephew of Winston Churchill (whose sister was Romilly's mother), he founded his own magazine, *Out of Bounds*, for fellow-rebels at Wellington and left that establishment aged fifteen, going at once to London and finding employment for a brief period in an incredibly grungy, not to say downright bent, advertising agency, where the staff's wages were cunningly redirected into the proprietor's pocket. When that enterprise collapsed he decided that the future must lie in nightclubs; for he held that the advantage of anarchism over Socialism is that in the former any endeavour is possible, since there are by definition no rules.

Romilly's nightclub was filled to capacity yet did not prosper, doubtless because his attitude to money was that it was stuff to be given away. At the same time as this venture folded in July 1936, the Spanish Civil War erupted, so in August, having auctioned all his worldly goods at his flat the day before the bailiffs moved in, he bought a bicycle and rode it to Marseilles (losing all his money, which dropped out of his jacket pocket, on the way). There, after earning a few francs working for a waterfront pimp, he got a passage on a boat taking a thousand young French Socialists to Valencia to fight for the Second Republic, and was sent to the military training camp at Albacete. Here they had to use sticks for rifles and, long before he had learned anything that he hadn't already been taught at his OTC, he found himself attached with eight other English speakers to the German XIIth International Brigade, the Thaelmann. This handful of men, not all of them young, were plunged into some of the most murderous fighting of the war, going straight from the Madrid front to finish the year with the Battle of Boadilla, in which all eight of Romilly's British companions were killed on the first day.

It is his book of that name, an account of his personal experience during hand-to-hand battles, which justifies Esmond Romilly's place in my literary hall of fame, and of which Professor Hugh Thomas, author of the definitive work on the Spanish Civil War, remarked that there are passages of which Tolstoy himself would not have felt ashamed. Romilly was nineteen when he wrote it, back in France, soon after he had married Jessica Mitford.

Speaking of his short masterpiece (I doubt if the text amounts to fifty thousand words) from a literary viewpoint, I think the secret of its success, its 'unputdownability', lies in his moving from the minor discomforts and embarrassments of being at the front straight to the horrors of battle. Thus at one moment the reader is with Romilly at the farthest end from the tailboard of a truck crammed with men when he is smitten with an attack of diarrhoea; and, the next, spread out in a field on his stomach with the same men, their only cover the tall summer grass, experiencing the first Nationalist bullets zipping towards them 'with a peculiar whispering sound, not unpleasant at first'.

There are wonderful descriptions, too, of the appalling muddle in the transmission of orders from the German-speaking brigade headquarters to the minute English-speaking contingent, their presence in the XIIth determined by the Republican command, who were convinced that 'German and English are much the same language'. That was one period when the interpreters capable of speaking German, English and Spanish (there were only two of them) had a really hard time, although, as Romilly pointed out, it didn't take long when you heard people yelling '*Fliege! Decke!*' to work out what that meant. As for feeling afraid, he says that he was afraid because it was logical to feel afraid, and that was that. But what comes through in *Boadilla* isn't fear, but a root-and-branch hatred of Fascism and fury at everything it stands for.

To provide but one example of his hands-on approach to life and war, my own favourite was when he was approached by a reporter from the *Daily Express* while he was digging a trench in front of the Velásquez building.

Reporter: What on earth do you think you're doing here, Romilly?

Romilly: I'm digging the grave of Spanish Fascism. What are you doing?

Volunteering for the British Army in 1939, he was rejected on the grounds that the War Office discouraged applicants who had fought in 'foreign wars'. He joined the Royal Canadian Air Force and was shot down over the Atlantic in 1942; he was not yet twenty-four. I would have given my eye-teeth to meet him, for he not only represented the generation immediately previous to mine, but was also a writer of exceptional brilliance with a rare capacity to present the most complex and confusing experiences directly, hilariously and unforgettably. *Boadilla* was received with rave reviews in 1938 (Esmond blew the advance playing roulette in Deauville) and was almost immediately snuffed out; it was republished in 1970, with the same result.

But then, after all, most heroes are snuffed out; but the fiery sparks they leave illuminate us and burn on.

CHARLOTTE CORY

◇

Charlotte Brontë

29 May 1993

*The novelist Charlotte Cory tells
the 'awful truth' about her villain,
Charlotte Brontë*

Nowadays biographers are delighted when their heroes turn out to be villains, but back in 1856 pity poor Elizabeth Gaskell. When Mrs G discovered the awful truth about her subject, she was too far on with her *Life of Charlotte Brontë*. The only way to avert a scandal which would destroy the very Brontë industry she was cashing in on was quickly to complete her whitewash job and get back to novel-writing. Fiction is, after all, safer.

Or is it? In Charlotte Brontë's murderous hands, fiction became a powerful weapon of character assassination, aimed with the accuracy of the deadliest Exocet. Vengeance is mine, clattered Miss Brontë, as she consigned her manuscripts to the Yorkshire post. Small, bespectacled, with bad teeth and a bad complexion, this overlooked spinster used her novels to get her own back. Publicly. Her strongest attacks on particular individuals are contained in *Villette*, the novel written when her literary reputation obliged her publisher to print whatever she wrote. How wicked, then, that one such act of revenge was directed against the publisher himself.

No one who read *Villette* in 1853 could have mistaken her portrait of a pampered, indulged son and his pampering, indulgent mamma for any other than George Smith (of the reputable publishing house Smith, Elder) and his mother. What crime had this pair perpetrated against Miss Brontë? Why, they had welcomed her into their home, introduced her to London's literati, heaped presents on her and taken her to the opera. Yet handsome young Mr Smith had grievously offended. He'd failed to respond to CB's complete lack of physical charms.

Charlotte Brontë was the sort of woman other women readily detect, the sort who throws herself at every man who comes into her orbit with a desperation and obviousness embarrassing to behold. As a governess she had been sullen, unprepossessing and obstreperous, the kind of *au pair* who falls in love with your husband, draping herself over him at every opportunity while openly disliking you and the children. Rather a pain, the real Jane Eyre.

George Smith and Mother came off relatively lightly – only fun was poked at them. Woe betide the beautiful women – the Blanche Ingramses and Ginerva Fanshawes – unfortunate enough to grace Charlotte's books. And, had Miss Brontë been as vituperative about Jews as she was about Catholics and Belgians ('the phlegm that thickens their blood is too gluey to boil'), post-Hitler's England would have struck her off the A-level syllabus long ago. And if she'd written *Villette* today, she would have found herself in the High Court facing massive libel damages.

She had spent a year in Brussels teaching English and learning French, and had fallen unrequitedly in love with Monsieur Constantin Heger, her headmistress's husband. Though Charlotte parted with the Hegers on friendly enough terms, once back in Haworth her infatuation grew unchecked. Over a period of two years she wrote this happily married father of five a series of increasingly passionate letters. When he did not reply, she directed the full force of her hatred against his wife. By teasingly substituting 'Villette' for Brussels and a whole set of names for other locations, Charlotte Brontë actively invited readers to puzzle out the true identities of her subjects. The respectable Mme Heger, whose school was accurately pinpointed, not only had to endure the devastation of being caricatured as the monstrous Mme Beck, but also found clamorous hordes of Brontë-lovers beating a path to her door. No wonder she refused to see Mrs Gaskell.

Monsieur Heger, immortalised in *Villette* as a romantic hero, received the mild-mannered biographer politely. He showed her Charlotte's letters, and she – whose sympathies, like ours, had been hijacked by the sad story of Charlotte's life – was shocked to realise what a vicious piece of writing *Villette* was, and what a nasty piece of work Miss Charlotte. For everyone's sake she agreed to gloss over the truth. But the Brontë industry need have no fear: who today would prefer the whitewashed heroine discreetly purveyed by Mrs G to the real villain that was Charlotte Brontë – bitchy, bigoted, vengeful, and morally perverse?

ANDREW DAVIES

Frank Harris

14 July 1990

The novelist and playwright Andrew Davies,
who wrote the television comedy series
A Very Peculiar Practice, *praises a man*
who strove to be 'the Galileo of sex'

In 1921 Frank Harris, sixty-seven years old, frail, broke and impotent, sat down in a Nice café to begin dictating his master-piece, *My Life and Loves*, to a succession of pretty secretaries. His purpose in doing this was threefold. He wanted to tell the whole truth about an extraordinary, rich life in which he went everywhere, met everyone and did everything. He wanted to establish his true greatness before a world audience (he saw himself as the Galileo of sex, a figure roughly compar-able in importance to Jesus Christ and William Shakespeare). And he was desperate for money.

Frank was born in Galway, in 1855, 'within the sound of the sea'. His father sent him to a grim boarding school in Wales ('nothing but fagging, frigging, and bullying') from which he soon escaped, using the £10 he won as second prize in an essay competition to buy himself a passage to New York. He was still only fifteen. In America he worked as a bootblack, then a night clerk in a hotel, which he left to ride the range as a cowboy, punching cows by day and reading Carlyle in the evenings. The life of the mind was drawing him like a spell, and he enrolled at Kansas University as a student of Classics under Professor Byron Smith. Smith was the greatest man Frank had so far met, in Frank's words a saint and a hero, but he was dreadfully troubled by nocturnal emissions which sapped his energy and robbed him of his vital bodily fluid. Frank advised him to tie up his unruly member with whipcord (advice he might have done well to take himself) but it was too late: the damage had been done, and the pro-fessor was doomed to an early death.

Shattered, Frank set sail for England, where he met other great men, all of whom confessed their most intimate sex secrets to him, often within minutes of making his acquaintance. Poor

Carlyle, who had never been able to consummate his marriage ('he just lay there, jiggling'). The great Maupassant, who sometimes had as many as ten women a day, and could summon an erection whenever he pleased ('You don't believe me? Then look at my trousers!'). Oscar Wilde, who was unable to convince Frank that buggery and boys were best: 'I have never indulged, Oscar, never indulged – though if Will Shakespeare had asked me, I should have had to submit!'

The trouble is, of course, that many if not most of his stories are exaggeration, unsubstantiated gossip, or straightforward lies; just as many, if not most, of his breathlessly told sexual conquests owe as much to fantasy as to memory. Yet they also possess considerable charm, especially when compared with the erotica and pornography of today. There is, for example, no hint of cruelty or violence in his seductions. His verbal techniques involved poetry, flattery, and pleading. He referred to the act itself as 'entering the gates of paradise' and, by the time paradise had been thoroughly explored, his partners were sobbing with gratitude and deeply in love.

Chance would be a fine thing? Well, not all of it was fantasy, not by a long way. No less an authority than Enid Bagnold, writing in her autobiography, confesses that she personally was taken through the gates of paradise by Frank Harris in a private room at the Café Royal, and that our hero was everything he was cracked up to be. Frank did have a strong appeal for women. Though extremely short, he was very powerfully built, and had an enormous moustache – a bit like Lord Kitchener cut off at the legs, as Enid said. But his eyes were deep, his voice was deep ('tones of gold and thunder' – Enid again) and men and women alike speak of his inexhaustible appetite for life.

And his triumphs in the world at large were not all illusory, either. He really did edit the *Evening News* and a number of other journals, with flair and panache, and he really was one of the first to recognise the talents of H. G. Wells and Shaw and Max Beerbohm. There is a famous Beerbohm cartoon, 'The Best Talker in London, with one of his Best Listeners', which shows Frank haranguing Max across a restaurant table. He probably was the best talker in London, but he wasn't the best writer in London. He wasn't a very good writer at all, though he tried and tried, and in his heart of hearts he knew it.

He wasn't a textbook Casanova, either. Far too prone to falling in love, feeling pangs of jealousy, experiencing self-doubt and depression. 'Nell, I'm getting old,' he wrote to his long-suffering wife, 'I feel it dreadfully . . . I'm desperate at times – still, I know a brave heart can win even now with my brains, so I'll do my best.'

My Life and Loves was denounced as a farrago of lies and smut. More importantly, it was banned throughout the world, though pirated editions of it appeared everywhere. Poor Frank didn't make a penny out of it. 'He was a man whose ambitions exceeded his talent,' as his biographer, Philippa Pullar, says; but he didn't let a little thing like that hold him back. He had a go, in his life and in his *Life*, and, by making a bit of a prat of himself, he added to the sum of human happiness. I think that's heroic.

RICHARD DAWKINS

◇

Pope John Paul II

9 October 1993

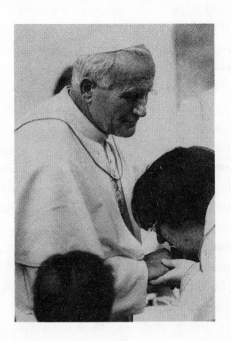

*Richard Dawkins, the zoologist and
writer, on the uncompromising heroism
of the Pope*

I recently heard a Roman Catholic nun rapturously applauded by an undergraduate audience when she expressed liberal, feminist, anti-Catholic views. Her opinions themselves were unremarkable. They were those of any civilised, educated person. What she was dining out on was the fact that here was a *nun* with decent, intelligent opinions. She was trading on the surprise value, the shock. Naïvely, I wondered why, given her anti-Catholic views on essentially everything, she remained a nun. It only afterwards occurred to me that, if she wasn't a nun, nobody would pay her train fare to express her bog-standard views. To do the honest thing and leave the Church would be to throw away her meal ticket, her one claim to be noticed. If she was trying to sabotage the Church from within, I apologise for impugning her motives. But in that case she was doing a less effective job than the Pope.

Pope John Paul II, that uncompromising stalwart, cuts a heroic figure by contrast to feminist nuns, atheist priests and trendy clerics who weasel the words of religion to make them mean whatever you like. The Pope doesn't mess about. He stands four-square by his beliefs and shows them up in all their extravagant absurdity: Virgin Birth (based on a mistranslation from Isaiah's Hebrew); Assumption of Mary's body in heaven (implies that heaven has a physical location and can accommodate physical bodies, which contradicts all modern theology, let alone science); Original Sin (God had his son executed for Adam's crime, a noxious idea even if Adam had ever existed, which, as the Pope's own scientific advisers will confirm, he didn't); Transubstantiation (wine turns into blood in more than a symbolic sense, so long as the officiating priest has testicles). No ordinary prelate could, with a straight face, re-prescribe such a rich diet of medieval baloney. In the late twentieth century, this is conspicuous folly on a heroic scale. Who needs an Aunt Sally when we have John Paul II?

The newspapers are full of snivelling modern Catholics, whingeing over the fact that the Pope stands up for his Catholic principles, demands obedience to himself and forbids contraception, abortion, homosexuality, embryological research and sexual enjoyment. They complain that he is illiberal, patronising, bossy, meddling, intolerant, bigoted, misogynistic, old-fashioned, dictatorial and ignorant. But what on earth do they expect? That is what the church they have bought into is *about*. It always has been. If you don't like it, leave!

If you believed in universal nationalisation and a workers' revolution, you wouldn't try to convert the Conservative Party to your opinions, you'd join a Socialist party instead. So, if you prefer family planning methods that work; if you favour equal rights for women; if you value the freedom to reach your own opinions; if you don't want a celibate old Pole overseeing your private life; if, in short, you disagree with the Roman Catholic Church, don't join it. And if you were unwittingly enrolled by your parents before you were old enough to protest, what kind of pathetic excuse is that? There's no Inquisition nowadays. Nothing will happen to you if you leave. Get out now. Join that nice Church of England, or another church, or none, or start your own. But don't blame the Pope. He is only doing his authoritarian, freedom-suppressing, thought-denying job.

The Pope's undeposable authority is the defining feature of the package you bought when you joined. In particular, if you want to be free to disobey, why, out of all the hundreds of religions available, choose the one that openly, clearly, publicly and without equivocation commits you to total obedience? Is the Pope infallible, or isn't he? If you think so, it is perverse to question his authority, no matter how daft his views may seem. If you don't think so, what are you doing in this church? Stop trying to have it both ways. Shut up or get out.

John Paul II is a courageous man of rock-like character, as befits his apostolic heritage. He heroically epitomises the preposterous institution of which he is head. He is perfectly qualified to do it the gravest possible damage and is in the strongest strategic position to do so. Long may he live.

RODDY DOYLE

◆

Charlie Cooke

21 March 1992

Roddy Doyle, author of The Commitments *and* Paddy Clarke Ha Ha Ha, *remembers his childhood* alter ego, *Chelsea's winger of genius, Charlie Cooke*

There was a boy a few years older than me who used to go from back door to back door swapping comics. 'Any swaps?' he'd say. He did it every week, like the insurance man or the milkman. He was a Spurs supporter. When he was asked what he wanted to be when he grew up the answer was always the same. 'Pat Jennings.' He didn't want to be *like* Pat Jennings, the goalkeeper from Newry with the foot-long hands. He wanted to *be* Pat Jennings.

We laughed, but I understood. When I was eleven I wanted to be Charlie Cooke.

Charlie Cooke played for Chelsea. My team. I'd chosen them because everyone else followed Leeds or Manchester United, and because my best friend followed them. I went through a lot of best friends then; the Chelsea supporter lasted two weeks and four days. I stayed loyal to Chelsea after I'd dumped him and he'd dumped me. We didn't support teams; we followed them. 'Who do you follow?' 'Chelsea.' 'Crap.'

In fact, I followed them nowhere. I'd never been to London; I'd never been anywhere except Wexford and Kerry. I'd never been inside a football stadium. I hadn't even walked past one. But I had a Chelsea scarf. My mother'd knitted it for me. The blue wasn't quite right but it didn't matter; it was a Chelsea scarf, the only one in Kilbarrack. Someone in the school yard tried to pull it off me. It scorched the back of my neck; the skin was crispy back there for days after. All for Chelsea. I could name the team and the subs. I knew their dates of birth. I knew how much they'd cost. I knew the names of their wives and children. I could put my hand over the top of the team photograph on the bedroom wall and tell all the names by the shape of their legs. Ian Hutchinson cost £5,000. Peter Bonetti was born in Putney. Charlie Cooke was five foot eight.

Charlie Cooke.

Charlie Cooke was a winger. He was brilliant. He was a genius. He was as good as Georgie Best and he didn't mess around with women. He was five foot eight, twelve stone two. He came from Fife. He was born there on 14 October 1942. 'He was a wonderful dribbler,' it says in *Chelsea: A Complete Record* by Scott Cheshire, 'often leaving a series of bemused opponents in his wake.' It's true; it was like that. Often, the opponents were bemused before he even got to them. They just let him trot by.

'Osgood. Now Hutchinson. Cooke!'

He was five foot eight. He made himself look smaller: modesty and cunning. It was the height I wanted to be; I'd be happy if I reached it. I was eleven and just over five foot. I thought I could make it. His hair was long but not that long; it was a length mothers didn't object to, my mother didn't object to. He was Scottish, I was Irish; both of us weren't English. He'd be thirty-two by the time I was sixteen, and I'd sign apprentice forms for Chelsea. He'd be a big brother to me. I'd clean his boots. We'd share digs. My mother would like him. He'd come to our house for Christmas because his parents were dead. I'd save his life. He'd come to my funeral.

One of my friends commentated on matches while we were playing them on the road. He was very good, very fair – considering he was playing as well. We had to tell him who we were before the start. 'Best.' 'No, I'm Best.' 'You're not; I am.' 'Charlie Cooke,' I'd say, always. No one minded. He was mine. I was him. I missed a sitter. 'Oh, no!' I said it with a Scottish accent. 'And, my word,' said the commentator. 'Charlie Cooke holds his head in despair.' I missed a lot of sitters. That was the difference between me and Charlie Cooke:

he was brilliant and I was shite. I was good at holding my head in despair. I practised it.

Chelsea played Leeds in the 1970 FA Cup Final. The first match was a two–two draw. The replay was eighteen days – ages – later, on a Wednesday night. I prayed for bad weather. Good weather meant high pressure and bad television reception. The day stayed cloudy and mucky for me. I got my homework out of the way. I couldn't eat my dinner. I sat in front of the telly with my scarf ready, a one-man terrace. For most of the game Chelsea were one–nil down. It was going to stay that way; I felt it crawling through me. I was very tired and cold. Then –

'Osgood. Now Hutchinson. Cooke! . . . And OsGOOD . . .'

Hutchinson stepped over the ball, Osgood kept running. Cooke took the ball and chipped – it took for ever – and Osgood dived and headed, and they'd scored. I ran out into the garden; the house wasn't big enough for me. They were going to win; they were going to win.

They won.

My father shook my hand. 'Well done, old son.' I'd won the FA Cup. It was one of the great moments of my life. I still think that.

Charlie Cooke ended his career playing for American teams called Los Angeles Aztecs, Memphis Rogues and – this one really upsets me – California Surf. I hate to think of him playing on the beach, watched by the cast of *Baywatch*.

'Yo, Charlie!' 'Way to go, Charlie-ie-ie!'

Jesus.

I don't know where Charlie Cooke is now. I hope he's well. I hope he's twelve stone two. I hope he's still leaving bemused opponents in his wake.

DAVID EDGAR

◇

R. D. Laing

3 June 1989

The dramatist explains his fascination with the psychiatrist's theory of madness

I came to R. D. Laing via a playwright and an actress. The writer was David Mercer, whose films *Morgan: A Suitable Case for Treatment* and *Family Life* demonstrated how people diagnosed as mad could, in their 'madness', challenge the suffocating certainties of bourgeois life. The performer was Patti Love, who had starred in a play of mine about baby-snatching, and who presented me with a copy of a book she'd read, with the idea that I might like to adapt it for the theatre.

The book was called *Mary Barnes: Two Accounts of a Journey Through Madness*, written by Barnes herself and Joseph H. Berke, a young American psychiatrist, whose other works include *Counter-Culture: The Creation of an Alternative Society*. Its subject was Mary's extraordinary voyage, with Joe cast variously as guru, guide and goal, through the wild topography of her lunacy. Mary's psychic Calvary took place between 1965 and 1970 at Kingsley Hall, a chaotic and crumbling building in Bromley-by-Bow, which had been taken over by the radical psychiatrist Ronald David Laing and his colleagues in order to test alternative means of helping people diagnosed as being mentally ill.

So, having contacted Joe and Mary and secured their permission to dramatise their story, I sat down to work my way through the Laing opus, and in particular the books that pre-date, or were written during, the experiment at Kingsley Hall. Many readers have adumbrated a particular progression in Laing's thinking: from the classic *The Divided Self* (1960), in which he seeks to make dementia intelligible, via the 1961 *Self and Others*, in which the psychosis is located not within the individual but in the surrounding familial network, to *Sanity, Madness and the Family* (written with Aaron Esterton in 1964), by which time he's pretty doubtful whether anything called 'schizophrenia' actually exists at all. And, come 1967 and *The Politics of Experience*, the thing's come full circle: far from being out of touch with reality, the 'mad' are in fact considerably more sensitive to their environment than the 'sane'.

There are elements of truth in this model of Laing's ideas. But for a playwright, what is much more exciting is a parallel (if dependent) development in Laing's view of how mad people communicate with the world and themselves. The brilliance of the early books lies in their perception that madness is intelligible. Thus, *The Divided Self* contains a justly fêted deconstruction of a classic 1905 case study of schizophrenia (Laing perceives that, far from behaving incoherently, the patient is sending up the doctor); it also contains much rich analysis of the life of schizophrenic language, including a particularly effective reading of a young woman's insistence that her name is Mrs Taylor, because, feeling cut up, shaped and sewn by those around her, she experiences herself as a 'tailored maid'. It is the insight that mad people talk and indeed live inside metaphors (as Laing's friend David Cooper put it, a delusion being a real idea which a psychiatrist deludes himself into taking literally) that makes Laing a great observer of the human drama, and a great source for those who make drama of a more literal kind.

My stage version of *Mary Barnes* was presented in Birmingham in 1978, and in London the following January. While researching the play, I talked to a good few people who had been at Kingsley Hall, but I decided not to meet Laing himself, fearful that – like kippers in the fridge – his presence would end up flavouring everything.

R. D. Laing didn't see *Mary Barnes* until 1983, when it was being performed in a Manhattan studio theatre so far off

Broadway that it was virtually in New Jersey. Straight from the plane, my mind greasy with jet-lag, I spent the first act trying to work out which head was Laing's and the second whether it was laughing or weeping. Afterwards we met, and he confessed that he had thought the play would be a more painful experience than it turned out to be; which I took to be a considered, if not a complimentary, response, because Ronald David Laing has spent much of his life analysing the extent and effects of pain.

In the same conversation, with more rue than despair, he admitted that a lot of people seemed to think he was dead. One can see why. The therapeutic ideas of Kingsley Hall have been – to put it mildly – modified over time (not least by Joe Berke's Arbours Association), and the evidence for some chemical component in schizophrenia now seems overwhelming. And the idea that the mad are saner than the sane has been relegated to the same bin as freeing your head, giving peace a chance and doing it in the road.

But, like so many ideas of that heroic if grandiose time, Laing's perceptions are still all around us. Most importantly, his work gave flesh to the notion that individual relations can operate as a paradigm of social relations, that the personal is both metaphorically and literally political. In that insight, as in many others, Ronnie Laing is still very much alive.

LUCY ELLMANN

Barbara Cartland

6 July 1991

*The novelist Lucy Ellmann
finds an unlikely heroine in
Dame Barbara Cartland*

Like a bride on her wedding night, I fingered the throbbing object with a mixture of fear, shame and repulsion. Could it be, I wondered, that a thing as small as this is capable of assaulting my purity of mind and my sense of the grammatical niceties and will indeed, under my very eyes, soon be ravaging syntax with practised ease? It was a horrifying thought. Yet the time had come, as it does for every woman. However joyless and painful the experience might be, I had to read a Barbara Cartland novel.

My reluctance was at once crippling and frustrating, my determination genuine. I picked the book up, and I put it down again. I lay back and tried to think of England, that bounteous nation which had produced Barbara Cartland in the first place.

Luckily, a friend was near at hand. Sensing my moral predicament, she took hold of the situation and read the whole book out loud to me. It was a noble, compassionate deed. For, without having ever read one of her historical romances, it would have been rather ungentlemanly of me to have used Barbara Cartland as an emblem of wrong-headedness in my own novel (soon to be written, as hers are, in the space of about three weeks).

Full of disbelief, regret and giggles, we followed Barbara Cartland into her pseudo-historical dream-world, in which an heiress survives the clutches of bucks, beaux and smugglers through the power of her personality, and the swordsmanship of a previously aloof admirer. United by a shared interest in horse-flesh, as well as a desire to remain within the aristocracy, they are soon exchanging bodily fluids, off camera.

The uninitiated reader might well pause when confronted by the various improbabilities, simpering eroticism and outdated attention to virginity. But the best-selling authoress is impervious to your scruples and simply pulls you along with greater ferocity.

For, grand, boastful, overbearing and silly though she may be, Barbara Cartland is also in some way right about women. There's enough virginity in us all to last a lifetime. We have no trouble identifying with her heroines as they search for a man who will solve those problems they don't even yet realise they have.

Her plots are scrabbled together more or less in the best possible order, and her imagination is unbridled, to say the least. She even gets in an ironic crack of the whip here and there. Her characters are camp, she has a new stereotype for every day of the week. She suffers from a pedantic urge to seem historically accurate despite carelessness over anachronisms. Her shameless bamboozling demeans the reader. But everyone likes to be demeaned occasionally, and her books are bought by the dozen.

She has served her public tirelessly, she has allied herself with several worthy causes. She has written more than five hundred books! The obvious question is: what's she trying to hide? What dreadful sin must be covered up by so many sugary books? Does she let a bit of her secret out in *The Odious Duke*, *Coin of Love* or, perhaps, *Cupid Rides Pillion*? (Due to my aforementioned disability, I am unable to carry out this research myself, but I offer my theory, free of charge, to her future biographers.)

This mysterious woman does not wear black or grey, but pink. Pink: the colour of girlishness, of lips, of genitals and Valentine cards. I suspect there heaves in her a mighty passionate heart, which aches to be surrounded by a passionate world.

That she must create that world herself, and create it again and again and again whilst dictating to her secretary, is the cross she has to bear. Once or twice a month, she shares her delirium with us. This is the cross we have to bear.

She is not a terrible writer, just a bad one who once had promise. *Stolen Halo*, published in 1940 and set in contemporary Cairo, concerns Doreen, an unprepossessing anti-heroine who has spent four years in a bigamous marriage, and several other years in rowdy behaviour with men at all-night parties. Her obnoxiously saintly cousin Anne conks out in Doreen's apartment, a death that is described in some detail: 'as her head fell back, a gaping mouth and open eyes gave an expression of idiocy to her face' (the author's hatred of this pathetic figure is palpable, and is pursued throughout the book). Doreen decides to impersonate her cousin. Abandoning the falsely identified corpse in Cairo without ado, she sets off to enjoy Anne's sober reputation in England. Disgust for piety, charity and goodness is frequently expressed. Redeemed in the end by her innate good nature (never mind the corpse in Cairo; just forget about the corpse, OK?), Doreen marries a good man, and sneakily vows never to reveal to him her true identity.

This is rather powerful stuff: Cartland sets up a heroine who will never really fit into any pretty picture, and she follows this fatally flawed creature through to the not bitter but ironically, daringly, happy end.

Is this the Barbara Cartland we have come to know and love? Or is this the work of a very angry young woman? And whatever happened to her and her anger? And how can we get her angry again?

ZOË FAIRBAIRNS

Albert Pierrepoint

16 February 1991

*The novelist Zoë Fairbairns respects
the executioner who changed his mind*

Albert Pierrepoint, the Yorkshire publican who from 1931 to 1956 also had freelance employment breaking the necks of living human beings on behalf of the rest of us, is still alive. He is in his eighties and very frail, living in a nursing home in the north of England. At least, so I am told by people who know him. Beyond that, they will not go.

Beyond that, I do not really want them to go. The investigative journalist in me is frustrated by their reticence, but the coward is relieved. If I knew where to start looking for Pierrepoint, I might feel I had to track him down and interview him, and I honestly don't want to. Just because I think the man has heroic qualities, it doesn't mean I want to meet him. Just because we have something important in common, it doesn't mean I want to shake his hand.

What the hangman and I have in common is opposition to hanging. Mine has been lifelong but always theoretically based – my life has never been touched by murder or its consequences. Pierrepoint's conversion arose from twenty-five years of hanging people, including household-name murderers, Nazi war criminals and an ex-customer from his own pub.

In 1956, eight years before the last execution in Britain, he resigned. He has never said precisely why, but in his autobiography, *Executioner: Pierrepoint* (published in 1974), he outlined the reasons that led to his change of heart. First, there was the courage of most of his hundreds of victims. 'If death were a deterrent,' he wrote, 'I might be expected to know. It is I who have faced them at the last, young lads and girls, working men, grandmothers. I have been amazed to see the courage with which they take that walk into the unknown. It did not deter them then, and it had not deterred them when they committed what they were convicted for. All the men and women whom I have faced at their final moment convince me that in what I have done I have not prevented a single murder.'

Not only was the death penalty ineffective; it was also, in Pierrepoint's view, unjust, because of the inconsistency with which it was applied. Reprieves were granted or withheld on arbitrary political grounds. 'The trouble with the death sentence has always been that nobody wanted it for everybody, but everybody differed about who should get off.' Executions, he wrote, 'are only an antiquated relic of a primitive desire for revenge which takes the easy way and hands over the responsibility for revenge to other people'. As one of the people to whom it had been handed, he gravely handed it back, calling the bluff of those who approve of executions as long as they can be carried out by somebody else.

Another noted opponent of capital punishment, Albert Camus, wrote in 1957, 'If society justified the death penalty . . . society must display the executioner's hands.' Executioner Pierrepoint displays his own and leaves you speechless. He was eleven when he discovered that his father and his uncle were both hangmen, and conceived, 'with a thrill of pleasure', an ambition to follow in their footsteps. After leaving school, he applied to the Home Office, was called for an interview ('Why do you want to be a public executioner?') and sent on a training course. This covered such topics as how to calculate the right drop, how to hang two people simultaneously, and what to do if the prisoner was upset or uncooperative.

Once a new hangman had passed the course, his name would be placed on a Home Office approved list. He must then await an invitation from a prison governor to attend on such-and-such a date (railway warrant supplied) and hang someone. It was a strict rule that hangmen, like nice girls at a dance, must wait to be asked. To volunteer to hang a particular individual was officially regarded as objectionable conduct, and, if there was one thing that the Home Office would not tolerate in its hangmen, it was objectionable conduct.

Other Pythonesque characteristics of the hanging profession as described by Pierrepoint included the problem of double booking (like airlines and hoteliers, hangmen were reluctant to lose a fee just because somebody didn't turn up, so some of them would accept two engagements on the same day as an insurance against a last-minute reprieve), and the mandatory holding of an inquest on a body to find out what it had died of.

When the state turns murderer, things must be done properly. Pierrepoint claimed to have acted as properly as the job allowed. He claimed a clear conscience. For years following his execution of Nazi war criminals, Pierrepoint used to receive a regular Christmas box of £5 from an anonymous person who simply wrote 'Belsen' on the accompanying note. Suddenly the gifts stopped. Pierrepoint assumed the giver had died, but nevertheless he went on wondering about the motives and feelings of the unknown person: 'Did he find peace?'

One might ask the same about the executioner who changed his mind.

MARGARET FORSTER

◇

Daphne du Maurier

30 June 1990

*The first 'adult' book the novelist
Margaret Forster ever read was
Rebecca, and she remains grateful
to its author*

Only once in my life have I been guilty of forgery and it was all the fault of Daphne du Maurier.

Every weekday when I trotted into the Carlisle Public Lending Library I had to pass a glass case in which titles for the adult section of the library were tantalisingly displayed. I would dawdle along, staring at the book jackets and feeling discontented with what was on offer in the children's section. My one ambition was to be old enough to belong to the real library, when I would instantly request some of those goodies in the glass case.

In 1946, when I was eight, and both tall and old-looking for my age, the cover of a novel called *The King's General* appeared in the glass case. Sometimes, when a new novel appeared, the whole of this showcase would be given over to other titles by the same author, and this was one of those occasions. There were four other book jackets alongside the new title: *Jamaica Inn*, *Frenchman's Creek*, *Hungry Hill* and *Rebecca*. I was not fond of anything remotely historical, so it was *Rebecca* which attracted my attention. The cover showed a young woman with sad and frightened eyes standing in front of a dark and mysterious house. I was completely hypnotised by it.

But there seemed no chance, for nearly another three years, of being able to get hold of *Rebecca* and satisfy my curiosity. I was stuck with Arthur Ransome, Angela Brazil and Enid Blyton until I was eleven and eligible to move to the adult section. The problem could have been solved if either my parents or my elder brother had been members of the library, but they were not. Nobody else read in our house. So one day, with literally thumping heart, I marched up to the adult counter and asked with that air of absolute authority, which was already my greatest asset if only I'd known it, for an application form to join. I took it home and forged my mother's signature, confirming I was eleven. When I returned with it, it was hardly glanced at. I was in. I had *Rebecca*.

It seems extraordinary but I didn't even notice the author's name. Authors meant nothing to me. I never thought of anyone creating *Rebecca* at all. I took it for real. I believed every single word – I was there, in Manderley, with the unnamed heroine, cowering under the glare of Mrs Danvers, walking terrified with her down the cliff path to the beach. The novel had a power over me which was quite crude and raw but it was what I wanted from a book.

Later, when I'd plundered the adult-fiction shelves as thoroughly as once I had done the children's, I thought how lucky I was to have begun with Daphne du Maurier. I was simply not ready for all those classic writers lauded so far above her. Soon after reading *Rebecca* I started Jane Austen (I was intending to go through the shelves alphabetically) and I was so bored I only finished one. The leisurely pace, the lack of anything happening, defeated me then. My reading was entirely undirected and unsupervised and I had no idea, pregrammar school, who was a 'good' writer and who was not. I took out and put back all those 'great' novels which should have had the formative influence upon me that they are claimed to have had on so many other writers: none of them mesmerised me as *Rebecca* did.

This discovery was to influence me in all kinds of ways both as a novelist myself and as a critic. It gave me a certain fearlessness as far as opinions went. I was confident about my own judgement and prepared to defend it. When a teacher said scornfully, 'You cannot compare *Rebecca* with *Jane Eyre*,'

I said that certainly I could. And did, though I deliberately overstated the case. I clung on to my refusal to be told who were the great writers and who the despised popular. I rejected absolutely the opinion, widely held, that truly great novels always require hard work from the reader. Rubbish. If the reader of a novel – a novel, not a PhD thesis – has to struggle, is made to feel stupid, then the 'truly great' is not great at all. It has failed.

I have never lost sight of that ability Daphne du Maurier had: the power to compel. She satisfied the primitive urge to be gripped, to feel involved. When reviewing novels I am always aware of whether that urge is satisfied, and if it isn't, nothing else quite makes up for the disappointment. The novels I read are often impressive, profound and brilliantly researched, and yet they are also difficult, leaden and ultimately exhausting. I return to them thinking how I admire them – and how I am not in the least engaged.

Roald Dahl is fond of saying the novel only has one func-tion and that is to entertain. It may sound as if I am agreeing, but I am not. It is insulting to the novel to suggest it does only this when, at its best, it can illuminate all those small corners of the human condition we keep hidden away, and in doing so inspire, relieve and challenge. But the entertainment factor must also obtain and there is nothing trivial in that. The more unpalatable the subject matter, the greater the skill and cunning needed to hook and hold the reader. It is a lesson I first learned from Daphne du Maurier and hope never to forget.

ANTONIA FRASER

Mother Ignatius

12 November 1988

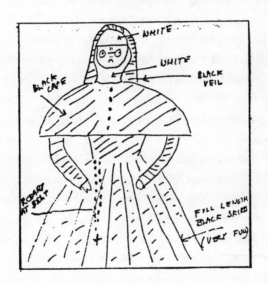

The headmistress of the author's convent school taught her that the glory of God was best served by doing a job well

My best friend from those far-off convent days at first turned pale, muttering something like 'so frightening'. Then she added more strongly: 'You must be mad.' This was when I told her that I was proposing to write about Mother Ignatius in a series devoted to heroines (or heroes).

Since Ig certainly was extremely frightening at times – if not downright terrifying – there is possibly something slightly cheeky in choosing her at this distance as my heroine, when she can no longer do anything about it. And yet it is also that passage of time, which took Ig to her neat grave in the convent cemetery many, many years ago, which has made me understand the measure of my debt to her.

Mother Ignatius was the first nun I ever knew. I was fourteen years old at the time, coming from my parents' donnish north Oxford home (no nuns visible to me in north Oxford), and she was the headmistress of the convent to which I was sent, upon my mother's conversion, with a view to being instructed in the Catholic faith myself. Ig's appearance was not particularly owlish; her face was notably blanched, even against the whiteness of the wimple which surrounded it; the corners of her mouth turned sharply down and her nose, too, had a downward curve to it, which gave her in profile something of the look of Piero della Francesca's Urbino Duke.

The circular black wire spectacles which concealed her small, very sharp eyes were, on the other hand, not particularly ducal; but they were the most menacing aspect of her appearance. Since these spectacles made it impossible to estimate exactly what Ig had noticed, one was left with the horrid suspicion that she noticed everything.

The teaching order to which this convent belonged had been founded by a remarkable Yorkshire woman in the early seventeenth century. The foundress, Mary Ward, was described by her fellow-nuns as 'a great enemy of ignorance', and that description would go for Mother Ignatius too. Not for Ig the kind of lackadaisical education generally thought to be suitable at the time for future Catholic wives and mothers; it was to the glory of God that one should be educated to the top of one's bent, as it were, just as it was to the glory of God that one should execute a Jacobean tapestry cushion without spotting it with the blood of clumsy fingers.

To Ig's great credit, she rapidly perceived that in my case God's glory was going to be better served by learning Greek than wrestling with the aforesaid cushion; a fairly obvious conclusion, perhaps (especially if you had seen the cushion), but not one which was fashionable in all Catholic circles at that time.

Indeed, anyone who could emerge from a smart girls' school in the Forties believing that it was chic to work owed a great deal to the headmistress. For, socially speaking, my convent was very smart, and for that matter Ig herself was also very snobbish, if snobbish in a romantic way in her fondness for the ancient Catholic aristocracy (to which I did not belong). In her references to certain high-born parents, she sometimes reminded me of a favourite story of my great-aunt, Beatrice Dunsany, about a social-climbing Edwardian hostess who, on overhearing a conversation about Machiavelli's *The Prince*, cried out lightly *en passant*: 'Oh, the dear prince!' Except that Ig, the great enemy of ignorance, would never have made such a crude mistake; there was little she did not know about Machiavelli – or indeed princes.

Professionalism was finally the great lesson of that convent's education under Mother Ignatius's aegis. Did I mention that she had an excellent sardonic sense of humour? I once announced publicly that I intended to work on the *Daily Express* as a journalist when I grew up; this was done deliberately in order to create a sensation – and thus gain the admiration of my friends – since the *Daily Express* was at that time banned in the school.

The next day after Mass she announced – equally publicly – that I was to sacrifice my entire free time to learning how to type by correspondence course, since this would enable me to pursue my chosen career as a journalist. The point of the story is not so much Ig's triumph as the effect her decision had on my future. Of all the many things I learned at my many schools, the art of typing properly is the only one which has been persistently useful over forty years, and has unarguably assisted me in my chosen career. Professional nun, professional teacher, professional wife and mother – even, if you must, professional journalist – but amateurism was not, definitely not, to the greater glory of God.

Years later, writing my first Jemima Shore mystery, which I set in this same convent, I used the character of Mother Ignatius for the headmistress under the name of Mother Ancilla (who actually taught us singing). Originally my 'Mother Ancilla' was intended to be unsympathetic, authoritarian, worldly and certainly frightening. But she ended up, I found, determined, humorous, a perfectionist and 'a great enemy of ignorance', being the true heroine of the story; as Mother Ignatius has, indeed, ended up as mine.

MAUREEN FREELY

◇

Father Christmas

21 December 1991

*A mother picks Santa Claus
as her villain*

Years ago, a friend of mine asked a very famous author who lived in her neighbourhood to play Father Christmas at a children's birthday party in December. He arrived late but in high spirits – and with a hip flask of whisky concealed in the sleeve of his costume. Having offered to share it with me and the other mothers – and found no takers – he opened his sack and proceeded to throw the presents about the room like so many Frisbees. When he accidentally clipped the side of one child's head, he tried to comfort her by picking her up and throwing her into the air. When my friend and I intervened, he invited us to take turns sitting on his lap. Many playful pokes and spanks later, we were able to talk him into going home, but no sooner had we got him out of the door than who should appear at the end of the drive but another mother, who also happened to be the wife of a Conservative MP. He took one look at her, let out a ferocious cry and chased her into the bushes.

We were able to rescue her, but our main concern was to explain his behaviour to the children. Father Christmas was very tired, we told them. He had forgotten his glasses at the North Pole and so had mistaken the MP's wife for a battery-operated doll. The more the children queried our cover-up story, the more elaborate it became. We knew it was wrong to make excuses for this man, but we couldn't stop ourselves. We couldn't even entertain the thought of telling them the truth – that this and all other Father Christ-mases were impostors.

Why rush the loss of innocence? We all remembered the excitement of hanging up our stockings, and our joy at seeing the presents he left us under the tree. Since these pleasures were lost to us for ever, the next best thing was to enjoy them vicariously. In other words, we were acting selfishly when we covered for the disguised author. We may have said we were trying to protect our children, but what we were really doing was protecting our own illusions about how nice the world looked when we believed in Father Christmas.

In fact, it must have been a far more frightening place than we care to remember. The whole point of Father Christmas is that he only brings gifts to the deserving. To get it right he must combine all the worst qualities of Jehovah and Big Daddy – seeing into every household, recording every act of disobedience and punishing repeat offenders by leaving them sacks of coal, while he himself lives outside the law. I put it to you that if, upon seeing the author chase the MP's wife into the bushes, we had told the children, 'Well, that's just the way Father Christmas treats women,' they would have accepted that excuse without question. This man is the original author of the double standard. The rest of us must knock before we enter and account for our actions. It's not the best message to be passing on to little children – that fat old men with noses like cherries who turn up at their bedsides unannounced always know what's best for them and so must be given *carte blanche*.

When I was five, what bothered me the most about Father Christmas was that he distributed his wealth so unfairly. If he cared about children at all, I remember thinking, he would give more to the ones with poor parents and go easy on the rich children who had plenty of toys already. So why did he do the opposite? A few years ago I told my own children, after a particularly poor showing, that Father Christmas had to be prepaid by cheque. But as I compounded the lie, I felt the same terrible shame I felt at the age of five, when I went downstairs to discover that Father Christmas had once again disregarded the ambitious list I had sent him. Like all believers, I knew there was only one explanation for his decision; he was punishing me for something I had done wrong.

What could that be? And there were other puzzles that were nagging me – how did he manage to visit all the households of the world in the space of three or four hours? Why did he have a different face every time I saw him? Why did his signature on the presents look so much like my mother's? I can't tell you how relieved I was when I figured out he didn't exist. What did upset me was that my parents had lied to me. What else were they lying about?

How good can it be for a child's first act of independent reasoning to lead him to the discovery of a betrayal? If he eventually decides his parents abused his trust because they loved him and wanted to protect him from the truth, he will conclude that the truth is ugly and that love means telling as many lies as are necessary to keep it at bay. He will slide without protest into the double standards of adulthood and then try to expiate his guilt every December by buying his cuckolded wife and hoodwinked children far too many presents.

Of course, I'll be right out there with him, fretting about commercialism while I match him pound for pound. I'm still in thrall to this unforgiving father figure who convinced me so long ago that I'm only worth as much as I spend on my children's Christmas presents. And you're trying to tell me he's far too jovial a man to think up such an insidious sales pitch? You'd better watch out: he's the devil in disguise.

CARLO GÉBLER

◈

Samuel Beckett

2 February 1991

The Irish novelist Carlo Gébler praises
the author of Waiting for Godot *for his*
integrity, his kindness and his humility

There are many writers I admire, but the one with the highest place in my pantheon is Samuel Beckett. This is not on account of his writing (value it as I do) but because of his personal and professional example.

When I first met him in Paris I was about thirteen and was enjoying a brief flirtation with clairvoyance and the occult. My offer to read his palm was accepted. Tracing the crease across the middle of his palm I pronounced, 'You have a very thin artistic line.' Laughter, I remember, followed.

The next time we met, I was going through a temporary infatuation with The Who and insisted he listened to my then favourite track on *Tommy* – 'Pinball Wizard', of course. I was delighted when he declared the music 'Wagnerian'. Even at that tender age, I recognised that his patience and courtesy were remarkable; most of the adults I knew would not have been so amenable, especially the famous, whom I had noticed tended to take themselves extremely seriously.

Beckett was Irish, born in Dublin into a prosperous Prot-estant family. A conventional upbringing – prep school, Portora, Trinity College, Dublin – was followed by two years as an exchange student at the École Normale Supérieure. His teachers at Trinity were grooming him for an academic career, but in Paris Beckett met James Joyce and joined the fringes of the older man's literary circle; when he returned to Trinity, he determined to make his way as a writer.

He survived on pin money earned from translations and hand-outs from his family, living first in London and then in Paris. He was just beginning to get himself established when the War came. Despite being 'apolitical', he became involved with the Resistance because, as he later explained, the Germans were making life miserable for his friends. After two years in the underground in Paris (during which time he narrowly avoided capture), he fled to Roussillon, where he spent the rest of the Occupation. He was afterwards decorated by the French government for his services.

In the early Fifties he entered a period of extraordinary fertility, producing first the *Trilogy* (*Molloy*, *Malone Dies* and *The Unnameable*) and then *Waiting for Godot*, which made him a household name.

When Beckett won the Nobel Prize for Literature in 1969, much was made of his relationship with Joyce. Here were the greatest Irish writers of the century – not counting Yeats – and one had served the other. (It is still widely believed that Beckett was Joyce's secretary – he wasn't, he simply ran errands for the older man.) Clearly, there was a line of apostolic succession; both, for instance, observed the dictum that writers must write about what they know. However, their differences are, in fact, more revealing. Joyce used his position of pre-eminence to encourage adulation and obtain favours. Beckett, when he occupied the same position in Paris thirty years later, did the reverse. He eschewed adulation and did innumerable favours for those in his circle.

When I was younger and more naïve I liked to think the artists I admired had an excellence in their dealings with the people they came across in their everyday lives, an excellence commensurate with their work. Of course, as I discovered, this was not so. Artists may be able to write, compose or paint works which are beautiful, but that has nothing to do with whether or not they are shits.

However, in the case of Beckett, both my own experience and the accounts of others testify to his being a man the excellence of whose work was matched by his private actions.

He was exemplary in his professional dealings, unfailingly generous to those in trouble, and tireless in the service of his friends. While he was no saint, he was certainly not a shit, and by virtue of his example I have been able to hold on to a little bit of youthful idealism which otherwise would have completely gone by the board.

Another major reason for respecting Beckett is his professional integrity. Every writer has something which only they can say and most spend their lives struggling to say it. Sometimes it is difficult to sing in your own voice; more often than not, no one wants to listen or they want a different melody. Beckett, like everyone else, came up against this, but he never capitulated. He stuck to his guns and, ultimately, people learned how to listen.

But what I admire most about Beckett is the position he took on himself as a writer, so at odds with the prevailing view that – as Saul Bellow puts it – writers fulfil a 'priestly function'. Beckett violently resisted this, to the extent that he was almost fetishistic about asserting that his texts contained no meanings other than those on the page (and were sacred only in the sense they couldn't be tampered with) and that he never had the salvation of mankind in mind when he put pen to paper.

In a world where not only are writers increasingly encouraged to be priestly but sometimes even end up believing they are our saviours, Beckett provides an admirable example of reticence, and one I would like to see much more widely followed.

VICTORIA GLENDINNING

◇

Martha Gellhorn

5 September 1992

The novelist and biographer
pays tribute to a fearless writer
with a sense of justice

Martha Gellhorn has always done what she wanted to do. That in itself requires more courage and energy than most people have. Very few people manage it. But what makes Martha Gellhorn heroic is that what she wanted to do has always been worthwhile.

In 1930, after her first year at college, she wanted to leave her studies and her happy, privileged family life in St Louis, Missouri, and go to Europe. So she went to Paris, where she lived among radicals and pacifists, developing the rage against injustice, poverty and the tyranny of governments that was to characterise her work. In 1937 she went to Spain to report the Spanish Civil War. From then on she has been 'attending wars', as she puts it, sending back her accurate, lucid, painful eye-witness reports: not only on the horrors of the Second World War but on conflicts in Finland, China, Java, the Near East, Vietnam and Central America.

Now over eighty, she has travelled to Germany to report on events since the Wall came down, and this summer she was in St Petersburg. She has always talked to ordinary people rather than the big shots; it is the wreckage war makes of the lives of the powerless that fuels her outrage.

Lots of things in private life make her absolutely furious, too, some of them concerned with growing old. She calls herself the Ancient Monument, and sees that this new status has some advantages. But she rages against problems with her eyesight, her back-pain, the hellishness of modern travel. Age has not mellowed her one bit. What she likes is information. A visit to Martha may involve thrashing out the iniquities of British and American foreign policy and the stranglehold of the international arms industry, as well as a nice strong drink and a lot of gossip.

In between reporting wars, she reported peace and its failures and betrayals. When she wasn't reporting, she was writing novels. When she wasn't writing anything at all, she was living. If she had not done so much living, she says, she would have written more books. Blonde and beautiful, she had – and has – a vivid personal life which remains very much her own business. Any journalist who attempts to describe her as someone's ex-wife, however newsworthy the someone may be, gets his nose bloodied.

She has made homes all over the world – Cuba, Mexico, Italy, Africa – and moved on. At present she lives mostly in Wales, on her own with cats. She likes scuba diving and reading thrillers. She hates what she calls 'the kitchen of life', by which she means domesticity and its dreary routines. For most of her life she has been on the job, on the run, eating out in cafés or living in countries where domestic help was cheap. Her cooking is shocking. There was something terrible she used to mix up which involved tinned tuna and sweetcorn. The only useful thing I have ever done for Martha Gellhorn is to introduce her to the miracle of the microwave oven.

Martha Gellhorn is unshockable and unsentimental, with a novelist's curiosity about her friends' lives. She has a novelist's shrewdness, and will often say the one thing that restores a sense of proportion. She can be tough as hell. She does not let you off the hook easily.

Last year there was a birthday dinner party for Martha in the upstairs room at the Gay Hussar in Soho, and when it came to the toasts everyone round the table said a few words about their friendship with her. All the stories were funny ones, about the hard times she had given each one either professionally or personally. Martha looked highly gratified.

Though her life would seem to be feminism in action, her attitude to feminism is definitely 'unsound'. She was less pleased than most writers would have been when her novels were reprinted as Virago Modern Classics, since she hates the idea of her work being consigned to a female ghetto. I sometimes feel that she has not quite got the hang of whatever it is that feminism has been banging on about. She sometimes has an uncomprehending lack of sympathy for women discontented with their lot who take no apparent steps to change their lives. She herself has always gone where she wanted to go and done what she wanted to do, so she cannot really see why all women should not do likewise, and all men too, for that matter.

Her astringent summings-up are delivered in a voice laden with experience and cigarette smoke. 'Nothing is for ever,' she said to me. This simple statement turns out to cover almost everything. 'Nothing is for ever' gets you through the bad times, and keeps your feet on the ground when the going is good. Such a comfort. I'm having it painted by a sign writer in curly script on an old mahogany headboard, to hang over the fireplace in my Irish house. There it will stay until its time, or mine, is up.

Martha Gellhorn isn't a mother figure because she isn't motherly. She is just herself. I have always hated the term 'role model'. It sounds like something made out of Plasticine at nursery school. I don't see why anyone should want to have one. In any case, Martha Gellhorn couldn't be a role model because she is custom-made to her own requirements. She is, simply, heroic.

ZOË HELLER

Elvis Presley

2 January 1993

The journalist Zoë Heller finds heroism in Elvis — even when he was fat and hammy

I can't remember when I first became aware of Elvis: he's one of those characters, like Mickey Mouse or Santa Claus, whom it's hard to imagine ever *not* knowing about.

Nor is there any precise date for when I became a conscious Elvis fan. I can work it out approximately because it was in 1974 that my dad's girlfriend came across an old pile of Elvis fan-club magazines while cleaning out her garage – and I had already been loving Elvis for quite a while by then. I was nine and Elvis was thirty-nine, with three years yet to live.

He hadn't sung anything with any real commitment for years. For a brief moment when he made his comeback in 1968, zippered up in black leather and sporting a pair of sideburns in the shape of isosceles triangles, he had seemed to regain the passion of his youth. But now he was fat, and given to wearing costume jewellery.

I loved him none the less. When my dad's girlfriend let me have her fan-club magazines, I agonised for months afterwards over how to display them on my bedside table: should I scatter them casually? Or arrange them in the shape of a heart? I settled, in the end, for sober, archival stacks.

The principal reason for loving Elvis was, and remains, his music. Elvis, at his best, was one of the most intensely express-ive and affecting singers the world has ever known. It was listening to his records – the early Sun recordings in particular – that I first understood how music could transport its listener. I must have heard those Sun songs a couple of hundred times, but they still thrill me.

I can *still* feel frenzy stirring when Elvis gets to the part in 'Baby, Let's Play House' where he warns, 'You may go to college,/You may go to school,/You may have a pink Cadillac,/But don't you be nobody's fool!'

In the years of loving Elvis, I have often come across the theory – stated explicitly or implied slyly – that Elvis's success was in some way tainted by the fact that he 'stole' his music from black R & B singers.

I have no time for this notion: yes, it did take a white man to make white America listen to black music. But that is a sad truth about America – not about Elvis. More important, Elvis did not simply 'steal' black music. He took elements from various forms – white country as well as black R & B – and created something that was entirely his own. When pseudo-sophisticates talk of the original Arthur Crudup recording of 'That's All Right, Mama', and suggest that the first, black version is somehow more 'authentic' than Elvis's, they merely indict themselves. Elvis brought to that song an energy and excitement that Crudup's lazy rendering does not begin to approach.

Now, I realise that there is plenty *not* to admire in my hero. Even at nine years old, I couldn't ignore certain distressing facts: that the inside of his Memphis mansion, Graceland, looked like a psychedelic whorehouse (the rooms had quilted *ceilings*); that he was on record as saying Pat Boone was a great singer; that in his later years his musical taste was shot to pieces – all these things were undeniable.

At first, like a lot of other people, I found the easiest way of reconciling myself to Elvis's lapses was to blame other people. Anything dumb or embarrassing Elvis ever did, I attributed to the evil influence of his manager or his hangers-on. Elvis didn't want to make *Roustabout* and *Blue Hawaii*, I told myself: Colonel Parker forced him to. It wasn't the King who chose those zebra-skin drapes for Graceland: it was his courtiers.

Believing this enabled me to fantasise about all the changes I could have made in Elvis's life had I been given the opportunity. If only Elvis had married *me*, rather than that no-good empty-headed Priscilla, I would have saved him from those dud movies and dud songs. I would have given him tasteful interior decoration tips. I would have seen to it that he ate sensible, regular meals and kept his weight in check. And the first day back from our honeymoon, I would have walked straight into Graceland and told that creepy bunch of sycophants, the 'Memphis Mafia', to scram.

Eventually, I recognised that I was kidding myself unnecessarily. The impulse to render Elvis flawless was understandable but fundamentally misconceived. When a person achieves true greatness, his other failings automatically fade into irrelevance. That is what greatness means.

In Elvis's case, I think, one can go further and say that his failings – the horror and pathos of his rapid decline – are actually a part of his greatness. If he had not become bloated and hammy – if he hadn't ended up squidging about on a Las Vegas stage wearing outsize Count Dracula collars – he would not have achieved the fantastic, symbolic status that he retains to this day. It was precisely *because* he was once young and achingly beautiful, and then became a sort of kitsch nightmare, that he was able to embody America's contradictory energies – enacting all that is both deeply exciting and terrifying in that country. In the end, there is something far more powerful and moving to be found in Elvis's last years than in the creepy level-headedness of today's middle-aged pop stars. Let them eat fresh fruit and grow old gracefully, campaigning for the rainforests. Elvis died slumped on a lavatory seat, filled with drugs – and still he lives.

LENNY HENRY

$\Diamond$

Richard Pryor

22 July 1989

A British comedian salutes an American
for what he has taught him about comedy
and about being black

I first heard of Richard Pryor at a shop on the Edgware Road called Tapes Galore. I was doing a TV series in 1976 called *The Fosters*, and rehearsing at the Duke of York's Barracks in Chelsea every day, but in the afternoon we were free ... Hurrah! So I would rush to Tapes Galore and they would indulge me by playing all the new funky imports from America. And I would bop around the shop in headphones having a great time. We are talking extra, ultra bliss!

So one afternoon, I'm in TG and one of the lads, a black guy behind the counter, is wearing earphones and tears of laughter are rolling down his face. He says to me, 'Len, I tell you what, you've got to listen to this, it's brilliant.' He went back, got the earphones, plonked them on my head and suddenly I was transported to another world.

I heard this guy talking with this weird accent saying, 'I hope I'm funny, 'cos I know if I ain't funny, niggers are ready to kick ass.' Also he did this routine about Dracula meeting a wino. The wino says to Dracula: 'You wanna suck what? You better suck your ass on away from here. That's what you better do! ... You wanna suck some blood? ... Get down to the blood bank ... I hope you get sickle-cell!'

Although to the uninitiated – that is, anyone from Dudley – the majority of his material was delivered in a practically indecipherable hip ghetto patois with colloquialisms, swear words and repeated use of the word 'nigger' (more of which later), I fell off my chair.

Here was a comedian who didn't tell jokes that were detrimental to his origin, who didn't feel the need to tell jokes. Although, I found out later, his material went through many drafts, test performances and honings, Pryor seemed to walk on stage and say exactly what was on his mind. He also appeared to be angry and fearless, a wicked combination for any comedian.

His material covered a wide range of subjects. From sport: 'White folks just won't give it to Muhammad Ali. Ali's kicking ass, making money and not killing nobody.' To marital problems: 'All I did was kill the car. My woman was gonna leave me; I said not in this mother you ain't!' To drowning: 'I was drowning! My kids thought it was funny. I had to threaten to cut off my kids' allowance before they would call me an ambulance.'

Actually, on the problem of Pryor calling black people 'niggers', he did kind of take it all back on his album *Live on Sunset Strip*, where he recounts the tale of his trip to Africa where he 'found his roots'. There is a revolutionary moment when Pryor sits down and looks around at all the different types of African person in the hotel lobby and realises that there is no such word as 'nigger', and that he has been using this very offensive phrase not just as a reaction against the white racists who used this slave name, but also simply to be hip. It is a stunning piece of work. Hearing him describe the moment as this voice appears in his head is quite poignant and very, very funny.

It's not fair to quote all his stuff. Really you should buy his albums. One of his best is *Richard Pryor's Greatest Hits*, which gives a fairly comprehensive view of who he is and contains highlights of all his funniest stuff. There's also *Is It Something I Said?*, which has a fantastic cover with Pryor tied to a burning cross, surrounded by the Ku Klux Klan who are dancing around. This man has got a serious sense of humour.

But the best Pryor album for me will always be *Wanted*. It's about ninety-two minutes' worth of state-of-the-art stand-up comedy material, where he goes through a complete range of subjects. From some squirrel monkeys that he bought, that actually put their willies in his ear, to Leon Spinks, to having a heart attack, to being in the woods, and nature. It's just wonderful material and if you can get it, please do, it sums him up perfectly.

But it was the film of the *Wanted* album, *Richard Pryor Live in Concert*, that made me want to do a stand-up film of my own, which I have done recently. It's called *Lenny Henry Live and Unleashed* and it comes out on 28 July (quick plug there, ha, ha, ha). When I saw his performance it was completely different to just listening to him. Seeing him perform the material, the way he uses his body like Marcel Marceau with an Afro, making different parts of his body talk, inhabiting the stage with dozens of characters, made me think Bloody hell, that's comedy! That's what I've got to try to do.

So I was, I suppose, directly influenced by him. And although I've never met him, I'll always be grateful to him. For instance his character Mudbone influenced my own invention, Deakus. His observations are sharp and inherently political, and his ability to do gags that seemingly have no punch line is a wonder to behold.

Pryor is a genius, and I don't use that word lightly. Just watching him makes me want to strive to be a better comedian, and to say more about being black, and, more importantly, to say it with honesty and integrity.

RUSSELL HOBAN

$\diamondsuit$

Walter de la Mare

8 August 1992

*The writer Russell Hoban
on the 'peculiar magic' of
Walter de la Mare*

I don't know that I'd call it villainous but it's certainly shocking: in the Third Edition of *The Oxford Companion to English Literature*, the only one I owned until this morning, Walter de la Mare rates less than an inch and a half. Margaret Drabble, in my newly bought Fifth Edition, gives him almost six and a half inches and tells us that he was born in Kent of well-to-do parents in 1873 and died in 1956, that he attended St Paul's Choir School, worked from the age of sixteen to thirty-six for an oil company, and is 'remembered chiefly as a poet, for both adults and children'.

I never met Walter de la Mare. Giles de la Mare tells me that his grandfather was of medium height, five foot seven or eight, and had a Roman nose and a high-domed forehead. He was interested in the supernatural and believed in a life after death.

In *True Ghost Stories of Our Own Time*, compiled by Vivienne Rae Ellis, his son Richard recalls setting out with him to look at antique shops one afternoon when a friend turned up unexpectedly and the expedition was called off. That same afternoon a woman who was at one of the shops the de la Mares would have visited told her husband that she saw Walter but she knew he wasn't actually there because she could see a bureau through him. Telepathy? Or was it an example of his uncanny ability to think himself into places? Even now, thirty-six years after his death, I'd not be at all surprised to see him in any of the places he wrote about, or indeed in this very room, standing by the window, looking at the rain.

De la Mare's poems are full of good things but it's his stories that make him a hero for me. He writes with that peculiar magic that makes the reader know more than what is on the printed page; whatever details he offers – Miss

Duveen's mulberry petticoats, white stockings and spring-side boots, or the immense coils of Miss Seaton's hair, or the 'grained massive black-leathered furniture' in the first-class waiting room at Crewe – unerringly bring with them the person, the place and the time.

Places always matter in de la Mare's stories; have a look at 'Miss Duveen'. Everything works from the very first line. 'I seldom had the company of children in my grandmother's house beside the river Wandle.' In the name Wandle we hear suggestions of wand and fondle and wander. Wands are used in magic; affection makes for fondling; feet wander, also minds. In this story there is, for a while, affection between a boy who wanders on stepping-stones across the Wandle and a lady no longer young who is, in a fond and magical way, somewhat wandering in her wits. The narrow Wandle becomes here the great river of time that bears all things away, the sound of it and the light glinting off the water intensifying the poignancy of the short-lived friendship that begins in a summer shower:

'It was raining, the raindrops falling softly into the unrippled water, making their great circles, and tapping on the motionless leaves above my head where I sat in shelter on the bank. But the sun was shining whitely from behind a thin fleece of cloud, when Miss Duveen suddenly peeped in at me out of the greenery, the thin silver light upon her face, and eyed me for all the world as if she were a blackbird and I a snail.'

But it is the shell of her own fragile solitude that Miss Duveen cracks when she confides to Arthur's innocence her sad little story of long-ago love and betrayal. She shows him a locket containing a miniature of a 'young, languid, fastidious-looking officer' and tells him, 'One thing, dear child, you may be astonished to hear, I learned only yesterday, and that is how exceedingly sad life is.' Miss Duveen, who sees angels in white raiment, is kept a virtual prisoner by her cousin, Miss Coppin; but the freedom of the garden is hers and the meetings with Arthur continue through the summer.

The boy, however, wearies of their strange excursions into the choked garden of Miss Duveen's mind. With the approach of autumn she appears 'in ever dingier and absurder clothes' and he begins to hide from her. Winter comes, and Arthur learns from his grandmother that Miss Duveen's friends 'have been compelled to put her away'.

There are moments and people in literature that become as real (and sometimes realer than) the moments and people in one's own life: Prince Andrey, in *War and Peace*, lying wounded under the blue, blue sky at Borodino with Bonaparte looking down at him; Ahab on that fateful third day of the chase when he hurls his last harpoon and, caught by the line, is dragged to his death by Moby Dick; Jean Valjean's flight through the sewers of Paris in *Les Misérables*; Hans Kastorp, in Thomas Mann's *The Magic Mountain*, running through the mud with bayonet fixed, singing '*Der Lindenbaum*' while the shells explode around him. With these I remember Miss Duveen in her defeat, forlorn and unchampioned by the river Wandle, made real for ever by the genius of Walter de la Mare.

NICK HORNBY

◆

Perry Groves

21 November 1992

*The writer and Arsenal supporter
Nick Hornby on the heroism of the
club's eternal substitute and its
most abused player*

When you are a football fan, seeing a new player for the first time is rather like meeting a potential in-law: someone close to you – your lover, your son, your sister, the Arsenal manager – is pressing upon you a relationship that may endure for years and years and years, and over which you have no control whatsoever. Such a relationship is inevitably problematic, particularly during the awkward early days. People try too hard, or not hard enough, and awkwardness becomes antipathy; before you know it, family reunions and midweek cup-ties become conduits for tension and hostility.

In the summer and autumn of 1986 the new Arsenal manager George Graham sold five experienced professionals of varying degrees of competence, and Arsenal supporters were baying for new, expensive replacements. We coveted Chelsea's Kerry Dixon, and West Ham's Tony Cottee, and Inter Milan's elderly but still brilliant Liam Brady; we got Colchester United's Perry Groves, bought for £75,000 back in the days when you couldn't buy anyone worth having for much less than £1 million. (The going rate is now £2.5 million.) He was ginger-haired and freckly, and his main talent was for running very, very fast.

It is a strange fact that when football fans bully, they only occasionally pick on the worst player in their team. Attitude is frequently regarded as more important than talent. Those with severe technical deficiencies can compensate by striking a rapport with the crowd (Wimbledon's cheerfully primitive Vinnie Jones is a notable example) or by demonstrating their commitment to the cause (Arsenal's Tony Adams, widely regarded elsewhere as a donkey, is lionised by his own fans). There have certainly been less useful players than Groves at Arsenal, but paradoxically his chief asset – his pace – ended up exposing him. Time and time again he would rocket himself past the last opposing defender, only to fail catastrophically in front of goal. In a sense, his commitment did for him, and consequently he became, in the strange phrase of the tabloids, 'a target for the boo-boys'.

Perry's genius was to strike a hitherto unimaginable compromise with the Arsenal fans. The deal was this: if he didn't play, if he could content himself with trotting up and down the touchline wearing his substitute's training top, then the fans would greet him with a variety of genial and genuinely affectionate salutations; if he strayed on to the pitch, however, then he was to expect the worst. Villain could become hero simply by staying off the field, away from the action.

Precisely how this state of affairs came about remains somewhat mysterious. Part of it was certainly due to Groves's irrepressible character; he never went to the papers with a MY HIGHBURY HELL whinge, and bore most of the abuse with patience and good humour. But more importantly, he just doesn't look like the whey-faced loser of football outcast legend. Originally dubbed 'El Pel', Arsenal's answer to the more celebrated 'El Tel' – Terry Venables – at Tottenham, a rogue tuft of ginger hair led to the nickname 'Tintin' (his increasingly experimental haircuts have been a joy). It is impossible to hate somebody called Tintin, and some kind of truce was inevitable from that point on.

In October last year, when Arsenal faced Benfica in Lisbon's awesome Stadium of Light, it became apparent that the relationship between El Pel and the Arsenal fans was becoming positively psychedelic. As Groves, the eternal substitute, started warming up on the touchline, a group of young men immediately in front of me started singing a very odd song.

'Number one is Perry Groves,' it began, to the tune of 'Yellow Submarine'. 'Number two is Perry Groves,' it continued. When they had got as far as number twelve, they launched into the spirited chorus: 'We all live in a Perry Groves world.' As in all the best poetry, the meaning of the song is simultaneously elusive and resonant, profound and strange.

A few months later, during an insufferably dull nil–nil draw at Queen's Park Rangers, Perrymania reached fever pitch. A large section of the away end spent much of the second half paying raucous homage to the great man – substitute, as usual, and warming up, as ever – who responded to these rather touching displays of enthusiasm with waves and smiles. 'Perry for England!' the fans chanted and, with characteristic self-deprecation, Groves chuckled merrily. 'Hallo! Hallo! Ginger genius! Ginger genius!' they sang, and his mirth intensified. His services were not required on the pitch that afternoon; but if they had been, one knew that these encomiums would have given way almost immediately to the more orthodox groans and sighs that had hitherto been his lot.

A recent contributor to this page found to his understandable distress that while he was composing his piece his hero had died. A similar fate has befallen me: in September, Perry Groves was transferred to Southampton for £750,000, his value having apparently increased tenfold during his six years at Arsenal. 'The fans never really gave him a chance,' said George Graham sadly, by way of explanation for his decision to unload. Well, yes and no, George; I miss him already.

PETER JAMES

◇

Aleister Crowley

27 November 1993

*Peter James, the best-selling horror
writer, on Aleister Crowley, who gave him
his first frisson of supernatural fear*

Two people really scared me as a child. One was the headmaster of my prep school; the other was Aleister Crowley, reputedly a cannibal, a murderer, a child sacrificer and a traitor, a man known variously as Baphomet, Frater Perdurabo, Ipsissimus, the Great Beast 666, and 'the Worst Man in the World'.

It was rumoured that after Crowley died his Hastings home was so terribly haunted that, within the space of a year, five families had moved in then moved straight out; and it was finally razed to the ground. My family home was just along the coast from Hastings, and for years the name Hastings filled me with a deep curiosity tinged with dread.

I never met Crowley – he died in 1947, the year before I was born – although I have sat in the chair in which he worked and which is now owned by James Herbert, the horror writer. It looks exactly the way you'd imagine the Great Beast's chair would look: tall and creepy and imbued with his presence. But I owe Crowley a debt for giving me my first real *frisson* of supernatural fear, because it is exactly the fear that I have learned to convey to my readers: that thrilling feeling of forbidden excitement which comes from sensing a twitch of the curtain into another dimension.

But was Aleister Crowley really the most evil man who ever lived? Or was he merely a mountebank? Or a misunderstood genius who was the victim of an international religious conspiracy designed to smear him?

He certainly possessed shamanist powers – once, for instance, making himself invisible when attacked by muggers in Calcutta (he later admitted that he had hypnotised the muggers so that they were unable to see him). He was a brilliant chess player, a fearless mountaineer, a talented writer and a profound philosopher. So what caused his own mother to declare publicly that she had given birth to 666, the Beast from Revelations?

What caused him to bite women when he met them? To persuade one mistress to copulate with a goat, and cut its throat during the act? To defecate on the drawing-room carpets of his hosts? To hang his insane wife upside-down in a wardrobe while he entertained his mistresses?

His rich parents were religious fanatics. He grew up with a deep-rooted mistrust of Christianity and, like the Knights Templar who turned to Satanism after witnessing acts of genocide during the Crusades, began thinking that when God had defeated Satan maybe the wrong guy had won.

Crowley believed passionately that magic was connected with the human will, and that man is a tragically passive creature because he lives so much in rational consciousness, bogged down by the trivial worries of everyday life. The key tenet of his belief became 'Do What Thou Wilt'.

Yet for all his Rabelaisian exhortations for the liberation of humans, he had, in Colin Wilson's words, 'almost no capacity for natural affection. It was this that made him a monster.' It was true, as Crowley's verse illustrates:

> Blot out mankind and give the beasts a chance,
> Nature may in their inheritance grant
> Some semblance of a race less infinitely base.

But beyond his lack of humanity, he became ruined by his addictions to sex and drugs, and by his gigantic ego. Ultimately he was rejected by everyone except the die-hards of the Ordo Templi Orientis cult of which he remained the international head, and he died, aged seventy-two, a lonely, bewildered, unfulfilled man in a seaside boarding house, muttering, 'After all I've done, is this the end?'

It is not, ultimately, the evil he did that makes him my villain, but the disrepute into which he brought the occult. For centuries, society has repressed occult practitioners and belief-systems in grim and paranoid ways. Modern doctors and scientists are beginning increasingly to realise that there is much to be learned by looking into our pagan past, where the roots of Satanism lie. Powers of hypnosis, telepathy, astral projection and shamanism play an increasingly important part in the way our futures are being shaped: in our attempts to understand human consciousness, to improve medicine, to help the mentally ill.

Satanism is a legally recognised religion and belief system on both sides of the Atlantic. I am not a Satanist, but I believe that Satanism as an intellectual concept should provide a counterbalance to religious fundamentalism. Crowley's crime was to debase the concept. He rewrote the laws of Satanism largely around his insatiable sexual appetites. As a result, all Satanist cults have become tainted in the eyes of outsiders, and the word Satanism has become a flag of convenience beneath which unsavoury organisations such as paedophile groups attempt to hide.

I believe that Crowley helped to blur the boundaries between the sciences of the paranormal and the worship of the devil to such an extent that even today, in 1993, any academic in this country professing anything other than a wholly sceptical interest in the paranormal is risking both ridicule and a jeopardised career. Crowley had the chance to further man's understanding of his existence; but he threw it away, and that was his wickedest act of all.

VICTOR LEWIS-SMITH

◊

Jake Thackray

9 March 1991

*The satirist and broadcaster pays tribute to
the singer and songwriter Jake Thackray*

It was a dose of epidemic parotitis I have to thank for my introduction to the songs of Jake Thackray. At the age of ten my musical diet consisted largely of the conventional anodyne 'Nellie the Elephant' type of children's favourites. But late one evening, alone in bed with the mumps and a long-wave radio, I tuned round the dial and found a gruff voice singing hilariously and enchantingly about Ulysses, a dog whose overwhelming, slobbering love is driving his master to suicide. Unfortunately, I laughed so much that my swollen salivary glands caused a temporary blockage of the trachea, making me choke at the very moment that Brian Matthew was announcing the singer's name, so for some time afterwards his identity was a mystery to me.

But a few months later he turned up on *Braden's Week* (the noble progenitor of *That's Life*), a Byronesque figure with the neck control of a rooster, enunciating in the clipped syllables of a Noël Coward and sounding as though his voice had been strained through five sets of adenoids. He became the show's songwriter-in-residence for several years, week after week producing songs that were unfailingly funny, disrespectful, bitter, romantic and dangerous in about equal measure.

I played Jake's LPs until the grooves wore out: songs dwelling on the infuriating, often desperate perversities of love; lustful blacksmiths; ageing spinsters; beautiful women with grotesque relatives; country girls longing for the Saturday dance; and jilted lovers drinking themselves into oblivion. Aged twelve, I considered myself pretty *au fait* with that world of seething passions, and longed to meet him to discuss the human condition further.

At seventeen, I got my chance. As host of my own terrible local radio show, Jake was lucky enough to feature as the subject of one of my famous celebrity interviews, conducted after a concert at the QEH. Although the stream of inane and vacuous questions I asked him can still remove the enamel from my teeth on the rare occasions I dare to listen to the tape, he didn't throw me head-first out of his dressing room as I deserved, but instead sat and talked for hours over a crate of Guinness about the French singer-storyteller tradition of the troubadours.

In particular he talked about his distrust of authority, of the law and the judiciary, and his loathing of bigots, zealots, swank-pots, and of pomposity ('Beware of whoever looks down on you from a height'), perfectly encapsulated in his song 'The Bull':

> The bigger the bull, *the bigger the bull*,
> The bigger and quicker and thicker the bullshite falls.

A few years later, as a producer on Radio 4's *Start the Week*, I was in a position to start booking him, soon finding that, like most geniuses, he could be the most difficult son-of-a-bitch imaginable to work with. After Jake complained that the five-star hotel I had booked for him was 'too grand', it became a matter of honour with me to select the worst hotels I could find in central London, and I often felt like going into the room before he arrived, urinating on the floor and releasing a jam-jar full of flies just to make sure. But it was all worth it. He produced some beautiful songs for the series.

The last time we met was in Scarborough. I arrived on my 1,000cc BMW motorbike, and Jake insisted on riding pillion round the town, asking only where my kiddies' stabiliser wheels were. We spent that evening on the tiles with Alan Ayckbourn, an event about which I remember nothing except continuous and uproarious laughter. Jake had had a front tooth knocked out in the car park after a rugby match, and next day performed a remarkable duet with himself, simultaneously whistling and singing 'Lah di Dah'.

I owe an immense amount to him, and clumsily tried in my *Loose Ends* radio pieces to emulate what he does so magnificently in his songs: identify the bullshitters, target them and ridicule them. I'm glad that, as *Braden's Week* was transformed into *That's Life* and speedily degenerated into a sickly mixture of crude seaside humour and mawkish self-satisfied litanies about cot-death, he no longer felt at home there. Had he been born in France, where the singer-poet tradition is long-established and little distinction is made between 'serious' and 'popular' music, he would undoubtedly be recognised as a major artistic figure. His own hero, Georges Brassens, straddled both worlds, being elected to the Académie Française for writing songs with immense popular appeal.

I have no doubt he is up there on a par with Brassens. Jake's songs are those of a craftsman: for me a perfection of form, with lyric, melody and accompaniment all interdependent and reinforcing each other. Quirky, left-brained melodies, quixotic harmonies, and a guitar technique which can sound as sophisticated as Villa-Lobos. We do not have an equivalent of the Académie Française. But we could, at least, raise him shoulder-high.

PATRICK McCABE

◇

Clint Eastwood

21 August 1993

*The novelist Patrick McCabe on
his hero, the actor, director and
self-parodist Clint Eastwood*

I first met Tyrone Guthrie in 1968. He put his head through a hole in the hedge and said: 'Good man.' I never saw him again after that. In fact, it was to be many years later before I discovered he was a bit of a big cheese in the theatre world. All I knew him as was Head of Raspberries, large quantities of which luscious fruit I was picking for him to put in his pots of jam. Throughout those heady, midge-ridden days beneath the open sky, my thorn-blitzed hands would whirr industriously in order that the fabled dramaturge's raspberry-cash would enable me to pay my way through Luxor College. Which, of course, wasn't an academic institution in the real sense or, in fact, in any sense, because it was a cinema. Not that the fees required were exorbitant either, but financial peace of mind was essential if other overheads were to be taken care of, not least among them Tayto crisps, Toffo mints and one or two bottles of cola.

And so it came to pass within the hallowed halls of the Luxor Cinema, on the day Engelbert Humperdinck got to Number One, that I encountered the man who was to become my one and only hero along this trail of tears we call life. The film was *A Fistful of Dollars* (1964), and he was telling some bad-looking bushwhackers that his mule didn't like being insulted. They made the very foolish mistake of laughing. Clint didn't like laughing. I'm afraid he didn't like it at all. As they soon found out when he said: 'My mule don't like people laughing at him. So if you'd kindly apologise . . .'

Sadly the bushwhackers thought this was the best ever, the idea of apologising to a mule, which was unfortunate because it left Clint with no option. They weren't the first he blew away, and they were by no means the last. I would say that, to date, the number of sidewinders and ornery critters Clint has dispatched would roughly equal my raspberry count over the whole summer all those years ago. But if people think that is all there is to him – plugging saddle tramps and bad *hombres* and mean dudes – well, that is just where they are wrong. The great thing about my hero is you can never tell what he's going to be at next. One minute there he is, blasting and burning and dynamiting, then the next he's having his leg sawn off by demented convent girls, with them all laughing at him saying, 'Let's see who's Mr Sexy now!' Or driving around Arizona with boxing orang-utans, or being chased by madwomen in California. Yes, with old Clint, you sure can have it every which way. You can have your dose of existential angst or whatever's going but you're always guaranteed a couple of good shoot-outs or busted cop cars as well. And that as far as I'm concerned is what art is all about.

Around 1972 or 1973, I have to confess I had a couple of dodgy years where I was going off the tracks a bit, starting to wander about with Kafka books and Keith Tippett records, frowning over *Last Year in Marienbad* (1961) and scanning cinema programmes for obscure Rohmer shorts and pictures with the end at the start. But luckily not long after that the outlaw Josey Wales saddled up and he soon brought me to my senses. When the bounty hunter says, 'A man's gotta make a living somehow,' and Josey goes, 'Dyin' ain't much of a living, boy,' I cheered, 'Good man Josey!' and our late-night common-room discussions on semiotics and the use of symbolism in Bergman became nothing so much as the tawdry, washed-out mutterings of a sad, parka-jacketed people overtaken by time and thundering hoofs.

Yes, indeed, the former Mayor of Carmel, Cheek-Twitcher Extraordinaire, mischievous self-parodist and, in his time, producer/director of as many turkeys as you can chase out of the farmyard, is for me a truly individual talent and conscience. Of late, he has been rightly honoured, ironically for *Unforgiven* (1992), which is as close to a feminist Western as we are likely to see. His name must surely rank along with that of John Ford, the two men who've shot the most varmints and sidewinders and in the process given us a handful of movies each that are destined to live for ever.

If Il Buono never smashed another cop car or filled another coffin, with what he has given us thus far he sure has made my day, punks.

SARA MAITLAND

$\diamondsuit$

Nancy Blackett

18 February 1989

*The feminist writer celebrates
Arthur Ransome's intrepid pirate
captain of the* Amazon

I don't think I have a natural turn for hero-worship nowadays. But when I was a child I had a hero (I despise the pale and unsatisfactory feminisation 'heroine'). One who I now see was a lucky and well-founded choice; a woman who transcended the restrictions of femininity without succumbing to the lures of male-identification. A hero who had all the characteristics necessary for the job, who lived between the countries of the material and the imaginary, and helped me to live in both.

She was Nancy Blackett, captain of that redoubtable vessel, the *Amazon*, who sailed the seven seas of a Northumbrian lake accompanied by her intrepid crew (afraid only of thunder and the Great Aunt). In creating the Blacketts and the Walkers, the *Swallow*'s crew, Arthur Ransome not only created a new genre of children's fiction, he also did me a magnificent favour.

I grew up in a Walker sort of family. I had my own John, the older, virtuous and caring brother; I had my Susan, the 'good' sister, who brought sense to our play. I had two Rogers: cheeky younger brothers who could charm the grown-ups when all went wrong. We even had our own Bridget, the family baby. I had a father who might have written the famous telegram: BETTER DROWNED THAN DUFFERS IF NOT DUFFERS WON'T DROWN. I had a mother who tolerated a great deal more than I like to give her credit for. So, of course, I identified with Titty: the imaginative, book-reading, dreamy one.

I needed a Nancy Blackett to change my fantasies into action. I looked for a real one, all over the place, almost entirely without success. I found her in fiction, which was the first great lesson she taught me.

The Swallows and Amazons books are out of fashion now – deemed by middle-class pundits to be too middle-class – but they were the stuff of my earliest literary life. I am glad of it, for they are extremely well written and deal with children who create their own adventures. The active excitement of 'making things up' and then making them happen is light-years away from the introspective passivity of much contemporary children's literature.

But beyond well-cast plots, witty dialogue and that pains-taking practical detail which keeps flights of improbability within touch of the possible, Ransome, by some inexplicable alchemy, created Nancy Blackett.

Nancy Blackett, at first sight, is just one more presentation of the stock character of girls' fiction, the tomboy, but in fact her creator breaks almost every convention governing this often suspect and dangerous female role model.

Nancy Blackett never wants to be a boy. Despising her 'real' name, Ruth, she picks a new one, but it is not a sexually ambivalent one, such as Alcott's Jo or Blyton's George. It is a perfectly good girl's name. Nowhere does Nancy express dissatisfaction with her female estate, only with the stupid restrictions put upon it.

Nancy Blackett is the oldest, the acknowledged leader. Her personality is so strong that even when confined to bed with the mumps in *Winter Holiday* her will and authority continue to direct all operations. Her infallible creativity transforms even the bleakest situations – as when John staves in *Swallow* at the beginning of *Swallowdale*, or when the Great Aunt descends like the wrath of the gods at the beginning of *The Picts and the Martyrs*. This is unusual: most fictional tomboys are either lonely, single children, or younger girls who want to be 'one of the boys'. They have older, male companions who are dominant, or they have sweet big sisters against whose femininity they are finally judged.

Nancy Blackett does not hold her authority over John and Roger by the old device of putting down other women. 'There's nothing absolutely *wrong* with pigtails,' she insists, when Dorothea's possession of these undesirable appendages is used as grounds for her exclusion from the gang. And although she affects to despise poor Peggy's terrors, she knows that, when thunder strikes, Peggy needs her.

Nancy Blackett never gets her come-uppance. The love of a good man does not lead her to take her own hand from her own tiller. In fact, the length of Nancy Blackett's childhood is considered to be a weakness in the books; right into their late teens she and John are galumphing around like ten-year-olds, rather than gallivanting like adolescents. Ransome, with almost unheard-of generosity in a man, leaves her unshadowed by the defeat (or the even crueller reward of becoming a 'noble woman') which hovers, like Nemesis in the wings, awaiting most such heroes.

At the end of *Swallows and Amazons*, after a night of terrified loneliness, Titty succeeds single-handed in capturing the *Amazon*. She is worried what Nancy will say. But Nancy, generous in defeat, claps Titty on the shoulder and says, 'Barbequed billy-goats, but I wish I had you in my crew.'

Ah, then I fell in love for the first time. Fell in love with all the brave women everywhere who want each other in their crews against all the odds of history. Fell in love with the power of female potential. Fell in love with Nancy Blackett.

She was my hero. Shiver my timbers.

ADAM MARS-JONES

◊

Michael Jelicich

15 July 1989

*The writer and critic remembers
his lover*

My lover Michael Jelicich died in May, of Aids, aged twenty-six, cared for by his family in New Zealand. I knew when we met that he was very likely to be ill, which raised the stakes from the start and made it impossible to keep our relationship casual. The virus helped our intimacy along.

Michael was in this country on a two-year work permit, but he didn't displace native labour for long. After nine months, in early 1987, he became unable to work, and I supported him after that. Michael hated to spend money, and took pride in how little his dependence cost me.

He often said that he was happier in London with Aids than in Auckland without, a statement that shocks me as much as it did when he first made it. But perhaps I underestimate the unhappiness of gay men in small cities. Michael was not attracted to the bleach-blond surfie in Day-Glo shorts who was, he insisted, the only isotope of gay style so far thrown up by his home town.

Michael was not an aggressive wit, a serve-and-volley wit. His was a quieter game, based on passing shots brilliantly disguised. I remember him convincing his mother, Beverley, on her visit to London last year, that people who wore National Health dentures found them embarrassing, since they had no division between the teeth, and amounted to a hoop of white, upper and lower.

Michael hoped to be a part of the first generation to live with Aids long-term. In New Zealand he had been somewhat New Age in outlook, a little mystical. He became more and more of a rationalist as time went by, but never mocked his friends' hopes or fears. I remember him saying to someone whose T-cell count had fallen to four hundred, 'That *is* low,' with only the faintest Victoria Wood inflection for my benefit (his own count then stood at nine).

It was one of Michael's achievements to disguise mortal fatigue with a relaxed manner, so that people could genuinely think he was laid-back, rather than dying. When he set his heart on something, though, he usually got his way – Christmas at a Norfolk inn, for instance, last year, though he had to ride pillion on a motorbike through driving rain to get there.

Michael had to leave the country soon afterwards, when his visa ran out. His unwise sexual orientation meant that finding someone he wanted to live with gave him no rights. He chose to go back to New Zealand in January, so as to enrol for university, but he was also keen to catch up with his family. His sister Robyn was sixteen, and had been fourteen when he had seen her last.

He was uneasy, too, about the prospect of being nursed by me. Even when a bug called Cryptosporidium had made him vomit in mid-bout of diarrhoea, he hadn't let me clear up. Now a cancer lesion in his mouth called for radiotherapy which would be debilitating, and he was more comfortable being looked after by Beverley.

Our household was also a little precarious. The flat I had bought in Highbury was small for us, what with Michael unable to work and me working from home. Having worked only as a hairdresser, he didn't realise that sometimes I only *looked* as though I was doing a crossword, and was inwardly refining some masterly phrase or other.

In any case Michael found what I wrote by and large tedious. Our relationship was not physically passionate, for a number of reasons including my fear and his exhaustion, but he could at least assure me that he didn't love me for my mind.

From Auckland he sent me audio tapes, until the inflammation of his mouth made speaking too difficult, and then he dug out his old typewriter. A central section of his pretty beard fell out, which greatly distressed him. Beverley fed him his favourite fruit sponges and crumbles, then mobilised her liquidiser so he could take everything through a straw.

Michael was by New Zealand standards a veteran of Aids, and made his voice heard. He was proud of getting the standard dose of one particular drug raised from 50mg to 150, after his researches told him that the relapse rates were much lower on a higher dose.

The wonderful day arrived when he could eat toast again, but soon afterwards he came down with meningitis. He was able to tell me on the phone from hospital that in his dark glasses he felt like Roy Orbison. He discouraged me from coming out to see him until he had left hospital; normally he won that sort of bet.

I still listen to Michael's voice on his tapes and marvel at the mixture of sweetness and dryness, qualities incompatible in a wine but not in a person, or not in this one.

Michael would have been amused by the idea of being my hero, but he might have approved in a general way. He resented the assumption that Aids was tragic largely because it cut short so many glittering careers. Nothing died with Michael except a few thousand expert haircuts – and of course the happiness he had from his friends, and returned to them.

ANTHONY MINGHELLA

◇

Johann Sebastian Bach

16 October 1993

*The film-maker praises the
passion beneath the austerity of
Johann Sebastian Bach*

I have in front of me a thumbed and coverless book of piano music, nearly thirty years old. I turn to a particular piece and find the staves scarred with fingering instructions in blurred pencil. Loud, one commands, and then, elsewhere, Getting Softer!: exhortations to practise each hand separately, an exasperated circle lassooing a passage where it appears the hands would inevitably crash. The pencil has ominously earmarked the page as Anthony's Festival Piece, Prelude in C, by J. S. Bach. The piece is simple, profound and intensely beautiful, written as a short exercise by this greatest of all composers. And I hated it.

Bach. Bach – just the guttural scowl of his name conjured, to the nine-year-old Minghella, exile to the piano room, mechanical drudgery, listless essays at what I adjudicated to be no better than scales dressed up as music. The trudge to Argyll Street in Ryde to be remonstrated with by my music teacher, the irritated tap on the edge of the piano case, Ta ta-ta-ta-ta, TA-TA ta-ta-ta-ta. Still worse were the sporadic visits to my parish church and the cold steps up to the organ loft, where, accompanied by the rasping lungs of the manual bellows, I would glue a fugue and clog the pedals as a faint odour of urine and displeasure issued from my teacher, an ancient imported from the more florid corridors of Gormenghast, probably as old as Bach himself.

I gave up the piano. I wanted to play football. Besides, there was the jukebox in my parents' café, stuffed with music made by people who were alive and rocking. I developed an encyclopaedic knowledge of the pop single from 1964 to 1974, and continued my musical theory in urgent debates about the merits of Hendrix and Jefferson Airplane and John Mayall and Van Morrison. When I eventually returned to the piano it was to pick out the chords to 'You Really Got Me' and 'She's Not There', and then later to make the crucial discovery that I could voice my own coiled emotions in songs, that I could say what I was really feeling, protected by the thick fringe of music.

Then, in my second year at university, I bought a record in a sale at W. H. Smith. It was, in fact, a boxed set of three discs on the Supraphon label and was incredibly cheap. I mention this only because I cannot think of a reason other than the irresistible allure of a bargain to explain what possessed me to buy Bach's Six Suites for Unaccompanied Cello, performed by Milos Sadlo. I certainly didn't know the music. I took the records home and put on the first side, the No. 1 in G Major, and inadvertently placed a bookmark in that page of my life. At the first cluster of arpeggiated chords, little ducks sailed up my arms in the manner of Popeye's Olive Oyl. An epiphany.

What does music do, exactly? If the pulse of soul or jazz gets the head nodding and the foot tapping, what do the lean sentences of a Bach fugue do, those undulating walks to the left and right hand? Why do I feel calmed, as if a hand were easing out a knot in my neck? Almost automatically these days, if I am in my work room, I listen to something of Bach's. Recently, during one particularly fraught rewriting session in New York, I realised I had left the Goldberg Variations playing throughout an entire night.

Bach is a no-nonsense composer. For all the ornamentation and demands on technique, he is composing in a time when colour is subordinate to line in music, when the noise is austere enough to locate the entire argument of each voice. Even his choral music has this transparent polyphony. He also wrote more good tunes, more thrilling tunes, actually more tunes than anybody before or since. The aria which generates the Goldbergs can appear disarmingly simple. But in the hands of an advocate like Glenn Gould (especially the second recording, just before Gould's death in 1980), it is revealed as heartbreaking, scalding, endorsing Pablo Casals' perception that, for all the rigorous and didactic character of his music, Bach is a volcano.

If my passion for Bach has made me intimate with some of his music, I know almost nothing about his personality. The only authenticated portrait, from 1746 by the Leipzig portraitist Elias Gottlob Haussmann, shows a sixty-year-old Teutonic man in a wig, strong-featured, but unremarkable. When his coffin was exhumed in 1894, it revealed a skeleton of medium size. He spent his entire career as a musician for hire, never perceived as belonging to the front rank of composers, steadily working his way from court lackey to Kantor at the Thomaskirche in Leipzig, a post he won because, as a local councillor grumbled, 'the best man could not be got, so we must make do with the mediocre'. He wrote a mile of music, he was celebrated as a keyboard virtuoso, he fathered a small orchestra of children, he made very little money. His widow was soon destitute.

What is evident from his life is a certain simplicity of purpose – an astonishing output generated by the requirements of the liturgical year, the imperative to produce and publish teaching-music, the opportunities to compose secular music for the court, and a lifelong fascination with the technical constituents of the keyboard, particularly the organ. Many becalmed modern composers complain of the difficulties of beginning to write, of even selecting a key. Bach avoided such problems by using the avalanche technique, composing a prelude and fugue in every key, literally hundreds of cantatas. And yet the music is never by numbers, there's wrenching pathos, overwhelming joy, a keen sense of drama.

Avoid me, I am someone who wants to share my passions. I made a film to celebrate the Suites for Cello and Clavier, I wrote a play to advertise the *St Matthew Passion*. I am liable to corner you and hum the theme from the slow movement of the A Minor Violin Concerto. I am that aggravating fan at the Festival Hall waving his hands over the score. And spare a thought for the eight-year-old Max Minghella, the next generation, stuck at our piano, scuttling through a prelude, unable to hear its song for wrestling with the incessantly streaming counterpoint. TA-ta, I insist, Ta-ta-ta!

BEL MOONEY

◇

Cleopatra

24 December 1988

The writer admires a woman who combined bravery, sexuality and political acumen

I have always admired women who are fierce, brave and splendid, from Boadicea and Joan of Arc to (whisper it) the cartoon-strip Modesty Blaise. I want the hand that rocks the cradle to be the hand that challenges the world, or dies in the trying – personifying what I see as the female spirit: infinitely strong and various, yet capable of great love (earthly or spiritual) too.

All those qualities coalesce in the idea of Cleopatra. A historical figure glamorised by myth, she dances through our collective imagination in the shape of a youthful Elizabeth Taylor, or prowls the boards as Judi Dench or Janet Suzman. Her lines are written for us by Shakespeare, and sublime they are – and yet the poet knew her no more than generations of angry Roman historians who vilified her name. All hand down *their* idea of my queen: proud and passionate lover or cheap, scheming seductress, doomed leader or easy lay.

The Roman propaganda is not surprising. They even said she had made a play for Herod, whom she hated; no ruse too vile for the oriental *femme fatale* who had charmed two of the greatest Romans of them all: Caesar and Antony. Their slighted wives understandably would have fuelled the talk. But the sex kitten who leaped from a carpet to dazzle Caesar, or wafted about on a perfumed barge to captivate Antony, did something far more serious – and far more intolerable to Roman pride. She it was who held the fate of the Graeco-Roman world in her hands. As W. W. Tarn writes in *The Cambridge Ancient History*, 'Rome, who had never condescended to fear any nation or people, did in her time fear two human beings; one was Hannibal, and the other was a woman.'

Not enough credit has been given to Cleopatra as a leader with ideas and ambitions of her own – enough to match any

Roman. Born around 70 BC, she was descended from a line of queens, but the woman Antony called the 'Queen of Kings' and who acceded to a weakened Ptolemaic throne was not in fact an Egyptian. This last ruler of her dynasty was Greek (with Macedonian, Persian and Syrian blood as well, but no Egyptian) and as such had to tread a wary path between loyalty to the Hellenistic world, which had no cause to love Rome, and the hard pragmatic knowledge that Egypt needed Rome. Her kingdom could only be restored to its former glory with the sufferance and co-operation of the Empire.

Schooled in the complex and often vicious rivalries of Egypt, Cleopatra was a political animal. An accomplished linguist with an astute financial brain, she knew above all how to survive. More importantly, she was possessed of a vision – one of the qualities Carlyle would deem essential to heroism. She looked beyond her own small country towards a Graeco-Roman empire that would no longer be under the sole domination of the Italians. Instead, the rulers of the Greek, Hellenised and Oriental kingdoms east of the Adriatic would be the associates of Rome, not merely, as hitherto, its subjects. Their status would be as equal as she felt herself to be in the love affairs with Julius Caesar and Mark Antony. It was a bold aim.

She might have succeeded. It is hard not to imagine, reading the accounts of Actium, that she would have done, had her Herculean Mark Antony been up to his mistress-queen. They argued over tactics (sea or land battle) and Antony showed himself to be weak, a vacillator, a man who hesitated fatally and all but lost his reason when he saw they were doomed.

Far more heroic was Cleopatra, who, knowing that Octavian had triumphed, spoke these words (reported by Plutarch, the most reliable chronicler we have) at the tomb of her dead lover, before her own suicide: 'But receive me with thee, and let me be buried in one self tomb with thee. For though my griefs and miseries be infinite, yet none hath grieved me more . . . than this small time which I have been driven to live alone without thee.'

Which brings me back to Cleopatra the woman. We know that she was not particularly beautiful, but fascinating and intelligent – the kind of woman who goes on captivating men even after her beauty has waned. I believe her affair with Antony to have been one of love, not expediency. For me, it is to her credit that she could combine romance with policy; because, in my experience, that is what women are like. They (or rather, we) operate on so many levels, moving swiftly from intellect to feeling, from aggression to acceptance, from self-assertion to self-sacrifice.

And so the enigmatic queen, whose image in stone or on metal tells little, and about whom records are fragmentary, lives for me: a strong, clever leader who could still admit the supremacy of passion, and die with nobility. Above all, perhaps, I am enthralled by her pride. Not for nothing did she see herself as the personification of the goddess Isis, whose widespread cult presupposed the absolute equality of my sex: 'I made man strong . . . I am the Queen of War. I am the Queen of the thunderbolt. I stir up the sea and calm it. I am the rays of the sun.'

PETER NICHOLS

◊

Bernard Manning

1 September 1990

*The playwright Peter Nichols accuses
the northern comedian of abusing racial
minorities and peddling a spurious
sense of Englishness*

'Are there any niggers here tonight? I see that one nigger who works here. Oh, there's two more, customers. And aha! between those two niggers sits one kike . . . two kikes. Two, three spics. One mick.'

That's not Bernard Manning, as you probably guessed by the use of 'kike' rather than 'yid' and the unlikelihood of a Hispanic turning up in Manning's Manchester club. Those lines are from *The Essential Lenny Bruce*, the point being that the words' suppression gives them their power, violence and viciousness and that, if you said them often enough, they'd lose their force and 'you'd never make any four-year-old nigger cry when he came home from school'. That argument seemed good in the Sixties, when Bruce was the only comic who talked dirty; now that everyone does (both on and off the stage), and children of all shades are still crying, it can be seen as only another fond hope. Although he was a hip preacher, a high-minded moralist, his laughs came from the use of racial stereotypes. His audiences laughed at the joke and at the same time at the awfulness of anyone taking that joke straight, in fact at the kind of people who thirty years later pay to hear Manning's cheery chestnuts about Pakis, coons, micks, Jews, Japs and queers.

'Blackie came into a pub with a parrot on his shoulder. The barman said, "Where'd you get that?" The parrot said, "Africa. There's fooking millions of 'em over there."' So runs Manning's patter.

He speaks in his own voice onstage and off, and never apologises. 'If they don't like it, they can go back where they came from.' He'd never find himself in Warren Mitchell's position – a sophisticated left-wing Jewish actor known more widely as Alf Garnett, the gentile, working-class Tory bigot with the stream of patter against coons, women and Labourites; a prediction of Thatcher values that was first made in the Wilson years. Taking his one-man show to working-men's clubs like Manning's, Mitchell found his spiel being so warmly welcomed that he sometimes broke off to explain that they'd missed the point, that Alf was wrong.

I have had my own taste of humour backfiring. When my play *A Day in the Death of Joe Egg* was about to open on Broadway, I was approached by the (Jewish) mother of the young actress who played the handicapped child.

'Sir, let me tell you how much I admire your play. I know it's gonna be a big hit but you wanna know something? You should seriously think of cutting the jokes about black people because, see, they gotta lotta muscle these days. Minority groups might picket the theatre.'

'But those lines aren't meant to be taken straight. They're ironic.'

'Oh, sure, and listen, between ourselves I agree with you – they should all go back where they came from – but they could harm the show . . .'

Manning wouldn't have approved of *Joe Egg*. Asked where he draws the line, his eyes lose their twinkle. He would never, he says, laugh at cripples or handicapped kiddies. Not even Japanese ones, no.

So the offence is in the intent and Manning's aim is tribal coherence. Does he approve of anti-Paki jokes at a time when immigrants are having fire-bombs thrown into their homes?

'Oh, aye. I've known what it was to live rough, you know. We could have done with a few fire-bombs in our house in the Thirties. We were perished.'

These days he's the true alternative comedian, more or less

banned from television by an official fear of his incendiary opinions. He expresses a point of view that I first met on my basic training in the Air Force, a few days after Hiroshima and Nagasaki. Most of my fellow-conscripts regretted the dropping of the atomic bombs only because it meant the war was over and they'd been longing to have a go at the Nips and Jerries. They cursed their lousy luck and hoped the next one would get started soon so they could have a go at the fooking Rooshans.

When I hear Manning's stuff, I'm eighteen again and back in that Air Force billet knowing peace is no more than a dream as long as we need the comfort of the clan. A few years later I was able to return to my sheltered life. My guard came down, I believed we'd said goodbye to all that – at least as far as my own countrymen were concerned. Then one day came the Falklands and the shock of learning they were all still there, waiting for a crack at someone. Argentina? Where the fook's that? Never fooking mind. We'll get the fookers. Conservative paranoia found expression first in jingo-ism, later in jokes, delivered by the Mannings of public life, alternative comics like Ridley and Currie. In their Führer Kohl, French poodles and Japanese-condoms-aren't-big-enough-for-Englishmen routines we see the false patriotism and post-colonial envy of minds that stopped nearly fifty years ago.

Time's against them. When Enoch Powell proposed giving 'them' £20,000 and a free trip home, the black actress Cleo Sylvestre was thrilled. 'I could buy a really nice house in Harlow for that.'

NIGEL NICOLSON

$\Diamond$

Robert Birley

13 January 1990

Ever since his schooldays at Eton, the writer and publisher Nigel Nicolson has hero-worshipped the late Sir Robert Birley, 'the greatest teacher that I, or anyone else, ever had'

'Now we are going to talk about the second most exciting thing that happened in ancient history,' began Robert Birley to his class. We were all agog, waiting for the most exciting thing (I think it was the collapse of the Colossus of Rhodes, or something like that), but the second most exciting thing was the Sicilian expedition of 413 BC. He didn't just teach it. He was Alcibiades in the assembly, an oarsman, a hoplite, a prisoner-slave in the dreadful quarries of Achradina, and the successive waves of enthusiasm, terror and despair in his narrative carried us with him. He was without doubt the greatest teacher that I, or anyone else, ever had.

My hero? Well, yes, but how much he would have disliked the term. As a junior master at Eton teaching history to senior boys, he was more like one of us, and we suddenly became undergraduates because he treated us that way. Punishment was something unknown and unnecessary in his classes. All meanness was expunged by his very presence. He mesmerised us by the exuberant flow of his erudition, shared with us his excitement at discovering, as if for the first time, the drama of a cataclysmic event, or bridged the disciplines, as when he made maths specialists do sums in Roman numerals.

In private, Birley was a shyer man. He would come to my room after dining with my house tutor, and lean against the wall, bouncing off it with his hands behind his back, his shoulders stooped, his great head nodding, and each of us was at first a little awkward. But then a sly question, a guarded response, or a book lying open on a desk would release words of comment or encouragement, usually couched in the form of an anecdote, for he always gave advice by example, not by precept. Once he started, there was no stopping him.

He was one of the world's great listeners as well as talkers.

Nothing would distract him from giving his entire attention to his immediate audience. A few of his chosen pupils would meet in his house – comfy chairs, a bottle of sherry, so welcome after the scrubbed boards and chipped enamel of school life – and one of us would read a paper, followed by a discussion. On one such occasion, he told me long afterwards, his wife Elinor was giving birth to their second daughter in a room upstairs, but not by any hesitation, a glance at the ceiling, did he betray his anxiety.

'Long afterwards' is another clue to my hero-worship. Robert Birley was the only master with whom I kept in touch all his life. He cannot have continued to know all of us, but with his astonishing memory and evident delight at rediscovering an old pupil, he formed a range of acquaintance that he enjoyed and exploited with undiminished zest. Never has a man played the old-boy network with greater skill or unselfishness, for it was always on behalf of someone else or a cause he had at heart, a poor black student, a crumbling parish church or a bombed baroque staircase, that he exerted his phenomenal energy and impish persuasive powers. He could squeeze dollars out of a stone. And he would always find time to reply, pages-long and in his own handwriting, to an appeal for advice on how an MP should vote on the Wolfenden Report or the European Referendum (yes to both), and for countless others besides myself he remained lifelong their moral tutor.

As Headmaster of Charterhouse and subsequently of Eton he was wrongly considered too much of an iconoclast. He was dubbed Red Robert, a sobriquet which originated, so his biographer Arthur Hearnden relates, in an absurd misunderstanding. A visitor to his office in Berlin, where he was educational adviser to the British zone in 1947, reported that above his desk was a framed photograph of Karl Marx. In fact, it hung not in his room but in that of one of his staff, and it was not of Marx, but of Brahms. But the legend persisted. Birley was not a clandestine Socialist. He merely wanted to open the best education to a wider social range, and argued this eloquently in the Fleming Report. He was determined to expose young people to a greater variety of experience, as when he invited Fenner Brockway, the left-wing and pacifist MP for Eton and Slough, to address the Political Society, which caused older eyebrows to rise in protest. Birley considered the public schools to be a training ground for future leaders, but he was a leveller upwards, a fighter for justice and human rights. Boys, he knew, can be pretty horrible, snobbish and cruel to each other, but he showed them that life can be more enjoyable if conducted more humanely and more adventurously.

I knew only at second hand of his later work as visiting professor at Witwatersrand University, where his commitment to de-apartheidising South African education was as great as his earlier passion for the de-nazification of German schools and universities. What a career it was! What an influence, on scholarship, on teaching, on liberal politics, on friends and pupils he had! He was knighted in old age, and nobody who was ever awarded the OM deserved it more.

CONOR CRUISE O'BRIEN

◊

Jean Jacques Rousseau

12 December 1992

*The writer accuses Rousseau
of being a bad father and a
detestable philosopher*

My villain has long been Jean Jacques Rousseau, and a most satisfactory villain he is. First of all, he has the necessary stature. Generally regarded as a great man, he has had admirers in huge numbers, in every generation, and every literate country, in the more than two hundred years that have elapsed since his death. This is no inconsequential villain, but one built on true satanic scale.

Second, the depth and versatility of his villainy are on a par with his stature and his fame. His personal life was villainous, with an assiduity in wickedness that far exceeds the normal patterns of sinful human behaviour. He had five children by his common-law wife, Thérèse Levasseur. He packed off every one of these children, immediately after birth, to the foundling home. Of this series of transactions, Edmund Burke, who saw Rousseau as 'the philosopher of vanity', wrote very prettily: 'He melts with tenderness for those who only touch him by the remotest relation and then, without one natural pang, casts away as a sort of offal and excrement, the spawn of his disgustful amours. The bear loves, licks, and forms her young but bears are not philosophers.'

Hypocrisy and effrontery have never been so successfully combined as in Rousseau's *Émile, ou Traité de l'Éducation*. This is a treatise on the importance of loving care in the bringing-up of children, written by the person who had dealt with all his own children in the manner described above. Nerve, at least, was something that Rousseau never lacked.

In every generation, Rousseau has captivated intellectuals with his fulminating aphorisms. The most famous is 'Man is born free but everywhere is found enslaved and in chains.' This is manifest nonsense, but it has mesmeric power over certain minds. As the literary critic Émile Faguet remarks: 'It would be equally correct to say that sheep are born carnivorous but everywhere eat grass.' Man is not born free; man is born a baby and utterly dependent. Rousseau's own babies were not free to avert their father's plans for their future.

Yet the maxim, intellectually meaningless though it is, has had the power of an incantation over revolutionary minds, in every generation. All you have to do is to strike all those chains, and man will be restored to the freedom which is his birthright. The thing has a beautiful simplicity about it, congenial to the arrogance of intellectuals.

All the French revolutionaries in each fast-succeeding generation of their number loved Rousseau: from the Constitution makers of 1789–91, to Robespierre and the terrorists of 1792, who destroyed the Constitution makers, down to the Thermidorians of 1794, who destroyed Robespierre. It was the Thermidorians who hailed Rousseau's *Social Contract* as the beacon of legislators. Their predecessors had seen that book in the same light. What a beacon it was, and what spectacular shipwrecks it has produced among those who trusted to its guidance!

The essence of the Social Contract is contained in the theory of the General Will. The theory itself is a complicated and ambiguous affair, but its complexities and ambiguities were important only in giving it an aura of mysterious authority. What concerns me here is its nefarious relation to power politics. That relation is quite simple. The General Will (whatever else it is) is an absolute, before which all must give way. So if you are believed to be speaking in the name of the General Will, you are wielding absolute power. Robespierre loved to speak in its name and when he did, people trembled.

The French revolutionary cult of Rousseau ended with that

revolution itself. But the influence of Rousseau did much to shape the intellectual history of the nineteenth century and the political history of the twentieth. Burke defined the French Revolution as the first secular 'revolution of doctrine and theoretick dogma' in history. The next was to be the Russian Revolution. The 'theoretick dogma' of the French Revolution was explicitly that of Rousseau; that of the Russian Revolution was formally very different, but in the spirit of Rousseau.

The germ of totalitarianism is Rousseau's notion of the General Will: the notion that there is a political absolute in whose name the initiates can lay down the law infallibly. Marx changed the name of the General Will; he was never one to acknowledge his debt to any predecessor. But in the Marxist system the governing absolute – whether 'dialectical materialism' or 'scientific socialism' or simply 'history' – is no more than a continuation of Rousseau's absolute General Will.

There is a connection between the villainy of Rousseau's personal life and the vaster villainies of totalitarianism. Rousseau was driven on by a colossal ego: it gave power and passion to his prose, and also an intoxicating aura of certitude. In later times every similar ego, and every power-hungry intellectual, has been attracted to him.

Rousseau sacrificed his own children to his ego, and his disciples sacrificed scores of millions of others in our own time. The evil that he did lived after him abundantly. What good he may have done I have been unable to ascertain. Perhaps it is interred with his bones, but somehow I doubt this.

DENNIS POTTER

◇

Ira D. Sankey

17 March 1990

*Dennis Potter hated Ira D. Sankey, the
nineteenth-century American evangelist
whose favourite hymns, collected in*
Sacred Songs and Solos, *he sang in the
chapel each Sunday as a child*

Sankey, the evangelist. Sankey, Sankey, Sankey. We all knew that the name had a sort of symmetry with the piece of cloth you were supposed to use instead of leaving silvery trails upon the wool of your jersey sleeve. But who was he? I could look him up in a reference book, I suppose, but the very prospect of even such minimal diligence provokes an unacceptable spurt of nausea.

No, let him stay as a booming echo reduced to a scrawled signature on the floppy orange covers of the Revised and Enlarged edition of *Sacred Songs and Solos*. It was there that I first registered his presence, and there that I began to blame him for the crucial first few inches of the gap which so soon opened up between every single one of my early dreams and every single part of my earliest realities.

Twelve thumping hundred thumping hymns (printed by Butler and Tanner Ltd of Frome) featuring 'most of the old favourites sung by Mr Sankey in the great Revival Meetings conducted by Mr Moody during their three notable campaigns in this country'. Inside the back cover are two advertisements, in a veritable riot of unrestrained sponsorship. The top one is for *The Christian*, twopence every Thursday. Each issue, it is promised, contains A Live Message On A Vital Topic, plus Sermons and Articles by Leading Evangelical Preachers and Writers. The other ad was for folding organs, especially built here at the heart of the Empire for particular ease in carrying from place to place, 'a valuable aid in mission work'.

These two announcements were the only relief permitted once one had made the thorny journey along Mr Sankey's narrow and yet narrowing path. Twelve hundred pieces, with each rousing chorus in italics, emphatically rhyming ultimate promises about the far side of Jordan or the hollow of His hand or the love under His wings where one's soul may abide. The old, old story. 'The story most precious, sweetest that ever was heard.'

Sunday upon Sunday, rain or shine, with polished shoes, scrubbed cheeks and clean hanky, I held this orange blaze of a book as a child in a small stone chapel on the higher slopes of a green and grey Forest of Dean, craning to look out of plain windows too high for anything but sky.

> Are you shining for Jesus, my brother,
>   Shining for truth and for right,
> Where bold unbelief and its minions
>   Are posing as angels of light?

This, apparently, was one of Mr Sankey's dearest favourites, a piece of information that enabled my seven-year-old self to get a first useful fix upon what could only burgeon into a properly sulphurous hatred.

> I'll soon be at home over there,
>   For the end of my journey I see;
> My dear to my heart over there
>   Are watching and waiting for me.

I cannot remember at what precise moment I realised that all these journeys were ending at one's last gasping creak, so to speak. The simple metaphors of trudging or labouring or voyaging had at first seemed as real as the folding organ. Winds blew, oceans heaved, roads became steep and stony, but none of these pleasingly graphic travails said anything particularly insistent about the great unmentionable.

Death. Oh, my God, is that what you . . . ?

Revelation of this nature changed the shape of the apple tree, and turned the silhouette of the coal shed at dusk into a malignant hump. Mr Sankey's signature on the cover of

Sacred Songs and Solos became more and more like the marks of a chisel on an ominous slab in the churchyard that nestled in old whispers against the walls of the primary school.

Somehow or other, and with a little twitch at the back of the brain which could easily turn into a much bigger shudder, I contrive to remain a sort of Christian. But in order to do so, against all the implacable materiality of the world and my own animal nature, I had to reach out from the depths of many a juvenile nightmare, put my hands around the neck of Mr Sankey (and his ilk) and squeeze and squeeze until the beaming monster had choked in his own allegedly radiant rhythms.

Alas, the bugger is not dead.

'Most of the old favourites sung by Mr Sankey' have this uncanny half-life that can still resurrect tatters and shreds of their chapel power in the corners of my imagination. Bellowed songs which mingle in the memory with the smells of boiling cabbage, the sound of rain on slate roofs, and the rattle of a penny in a wooden collecting box.

> In the silent midnight watches,
>   List – thy bosom's door!
> How it knocketh, knocketh, knocketh,
>   Knocketh, evermore!
> Say not 'tis thy pulse beating –
>   'Tis thy heart of sin;
> 'Tis thy Saviour knocks, and crieth
>   'Rise, and let Me in!'

Quarter-way through an adult snigger, my scalp tingles. It is not the witty and heroic Galilean at the door. Mr Sankey is upon the threshold, with an evangelist's ever-accusing grin upon his slavering lip, brandishing a floppy orange book. Dear God. Sweet Jesus. No, no, no . . .

KATE PULLINGER

$\Diamond$

Dracula

24 June 1989

*The young Canadian-born
novelist is fascinated by a
sexually attractive vampire*

'There was a deliberate voluptuousness which was both thrill-ing and repulsive, and as she arched her neck she actually licked her lips like an animal, till I could see in the moonlight the moisture shining on the scarlet lips and on the red tongue as it lapped the white, sharp teeth.' Jonathan Harker, the mild-mannered solicitor in Bram Stoker's *Dracula*, is about to be set upon by three female vampires. In an agony of delicious confusion, he longs for them to bite his throat, knowing full well where that will lead.

When I was a pubescent little girl I developed an abiding fascination with the vampire, one of our most complicated, exploited and familiar cultural projections. As a teenager I read Stoker's book and it remains the only Victorian novel in which I've ever wished to be a character. I think *Dracula* contains several of the most sexually charged passages ever written, as well as several of the most frightening. And the count himself, tantalisingly introduced early on and then appearing only once or twice in the rest of the book, is the most powerful creation of fiction, a truly dark, sexy figure to be feared and desired simultaneously.

Stoker did not invent the vampire; the legends were well known throughout Europe and elsewhere long before his time. Most cultures seem to have some kind of vampiric bogeyman creature that sucks the life-blood from loved ones during the night. Potted psychological anthropology is unnecessary; even at thirteen I knew that this figure was somehow tied up with my own feelings of guilt, hate, lust, and the fear of death.

Ever since *Nosferatu* held silent film-goers by the throat in 1922, *Dracula* has been remade countless times for the cinema. There is an enormous wealth of non-*Dracula*-based vampire movies as well; in fact, over the years the vampire movie has gone from horror to parody and back again, with Abbott and Costello and George Romero's *Martin* at opposite ends of the spectrum. We are currently seeing new life in the genre with films such as *Near Dark*, Kathryn Bigelow's tale of a family of vampire punks and hippies driving around California.

Good vampire movies give new currency to something familiar, sucking fresh blood from tired old plots. The vampire has proved much more durable than any other Hollywood monster. (Even with the zombie film there is only a limited amount of bandage with which to run.) The vampire is intelligent, attractive and lethal, a combination than not even *Elm Street*'s Freddie Krueger can rival.

One of the most appealing things about the vampire is that it is not exclusively male nor is it always heterosexually inclined. There have been many female vampires in the past and, although I'll admit that most lesbian vampires have been intended for heterosexual titillation, at least they are allowed to exist. In its female incarnation the vampire is doubly potent as a symbol and, in a way, this is one of the few places in popular culture where female sexuality is granted the complexity it is due.

Baudelaire composed several vampire poems, Goethe wrote 'The Bride of Corinth', while Keats, Dumas, Tolstoy, Poe, Byron – himself a vampiric figure in the popular mind – and, more recently, Anne Rice and Stephen King have all had a go at invoking the 'beautiful monster'. We all know about vampires and even the most disbelieving and uninterested knows to resort to the crucifix, the garlic and the holy water in case of attack.

The Christian Church has always played an important part in the particular little manifestation of our collective nightmare where 'The Blood is the Life!' in more ways than one. Some scholars – like, for instance, Montagu Summers, the famous vampirologist and social anthropologist, a man who actually believed in the existence of vampires and was proud to admit it – maintain that in the seventeenth century the Roman Catholic Church encouraged peasant belief in the vampire and, by extension, in the power of Catholic symbolism to ward off the Ottoman threat in Central Europe (symbolised by Transylvania).

And yet what is so appealing about an undead creature who rises nightly from the grave to look for willing victims to suck the very blood from their veins?

In *Totem and Taboo* Freud says, 'It was from corpses that the concept of evil spirits first arose.' My own fascination with the vampire is not so much to do with the fear of death, although I do fear it, nor the fear of dead people. For me, the thing I admire most about the count is his sexiness, the way that he and 'his kind' can reduce even the most dull and upright person to a quivering mass of voluptuous desire through some dark and inexplicable power. Like the vampire itself, the myth will never die; it will go on mutating and reappear in new, more, or perhaps less, recognisable forms. That is why the vampire is my hero; it's a kind of Teflon metaphor: whatever you do to it, it will rise again, gleaming.

MICHÈLE ROBERTS

◇

Colette

26 September 1992

*Michèle Roberts praises
Colette (1873–1954) for
her powerful femininity*

Colette would have smiled at the idea of writing about either a hero or a villain. Her characters are as simple and as complex in their hungers and desires as she herself seems to have been, operating beyond the sort of morality which divides acts and people into better or worse.

So she might laugh, if she cared at all, at being claimed as a heroine, since her life contained all sorts of escapades which shocked the strait-laced among her contemporaries before they finally turned her into a national monument and glossed over certain bits of her biography: nude appearances in music-hall tableaux, love affairs with other women, attendance at modernist lesbian salons, an impoverished vagabond life as an actress, a love affair with her adolescent stepson, marriage to a much younger man. It is those same episodes which have constructed her in English eyes as a symbol of 1890s decadence, a chronicler of schoolgirl perversities, a naughty bit of Parisian fluff.

Once I'd read beyond the early Claudine novels (produced when Willy, Colette's first husband, locked her up until she wrote for her supper; he subsequently paraded her as his pet and pocketed the cash), had got into the later novels, where she invents a language as supple and exciting as her own gymnast's body, and had devoured volumes of her letters and all the biographies I could find, I discovered that Colette did represent a heroine for me. She lived at the centre of her turbulent life with wit and integrity; she supported herself by her writing; she demonstrated that creativity came not from loss but from a joyful connection to sensuality, to the body, to the earth and all its fruits; she passionately loved her women friends while pursuing her male lovers; she wrote as a woman, eyes open upon the whole world of female experience, without ever anguishing that to be a woman writer was to be somehow limited.

Her works laugh in the face of pompous theories of women's penis envy, of female lack. Feminine, when I apply the word to Colette, means: powerful, erotic (connected), honest, adventurous, greedy, earthy, professional. I'd have to add: and sometimes cruel. She did abruptly abandon her woman lover Missy to go off with the politician Henri de Jouvenel, who became her second husband. She doesn't seem to have been a good mother to her daughter Bel-Gazou. She did base a short novel on a woman lover against the latter's expressed wishes. She was not, thanks be to the pagan gods of her native Burgundy, a plaster saint.

The presiding goddess of Colette's childhood was her mother, Sido, the countrywoman who took her dog to Mass, who read Corneille's plays concealed inside her missal during the sermon, who upbraided the priest for the way he taught the children religion and then gracefully accepted a handful of cuttings from his best plants, who calmly ate her breakfast while relishing the sight of her neighbour's barn burning to the ground, who waved her daughter off to the woods at dawn, who was full of unsentimental country lore and wisdom, who was sharp with Colette about not wasting her talent as a writer. Sido was possessive, resenting her children's marriages more than their love affairs (she always sent her love to Missy). She called her daughter her treasure, her masterpiece, she called her Minet-Chéri. A paradise, then, Colette's childhood as she reimagined it: no Oedipal serpent; a shy, loving father, and two wild brothers as playmates.

If Colette had written only those novels (or sketches – what to call these forms she invents?) of Sido, and none of the many other novels and short stories in which she relishes language keenly as the *haute cuisine* she finally grew fat on, I'd still think her a heroine for providing us with apparently simple but, in fact, highly sophisticated literary images of what deep love between a mother and daughter can be like. We have so few. Sido's love seems to have grounded Colette in a knowledge of her own worth and creativity, in an understanding that this first great love for her mother (homosexuality as a woman's birthright) would colour all her subsequent attachments. She had no shame in allowing adult passion to have its maternal, its sisterly, its incestuous aspects. She had no need to bother with categories such as pure and impure.

It is tempting for me to idealise Colette and then to envy her, to mourn my difference from the heroine I've invented, let alone grind my teeth over the beautiful prose-webs she weaves, the images of wholeness she produces. I, too, have a French mother; I, too, spent a formative part of my childhood in what was then an idyllic French rural landscape. But I ended up writing about split women, not whole ones, women torn apart inside by warring bits of themselves, women whose desire was often mixed with anger. Nasty girl. Bad sister.

Colette waves me on, though, as I move into my forties, grow closer to my mother, discover what unites as well as what separates us, sit together sometimes for long and loving chats, exchange recipes. That goddess and that paradise, well, they come and go and then come back. The need to work hard at writing remains. Thanks, Colette.

ANTONY SHER

◊

Eugene Terre'Blanche

25 April 1992

*The actor and novelist is fascinated
by his sworn enemy, the leader of
South Africa's far right*

Eugene Terre'Blanche, leader of South Africa's far-right Afrikaner resistance movement (AWB), did me a great favour recently – he helped me win an old family battle.

Whenever I go back to South Africa, I end up squabbling with my family, despite all resolutions to 'keep off politics'. I always lose these fights, ground down by the particular way my family have condoned apartheid over the years, through silence (often not voting in elections), or by convincing themselves that things weren't as bad as the world thought.

Like most of South Africa's Jews, my family have lived there during this century without noticing anything familiar. They never ventured near the ghettos known as townships, never protested at the murderous persecution around them. No, it was their turn to close their eyes and bask in the sun. Until Terre'Blanche came along. Suddenly my family saw something they recognised – the swastika above his head – and it shocked them so deeply that at De Klerk's recent make-or-break referendum they were stampeding the ballot-box to vote 'Yes' for reform. Terre'Blanche had finally politicised them.

I find myself irresistibly drawn towards him, as I am to Hitler. I'll watch any documentary which features them, I'll read every book. And a Hitler/Terre'Blanche figure crops up regularly in my own work. He's there in roles like Richard III, Arturo Ui or Tamburlaine, and he's there in both of my novels: in *Middlepost*, Terre'Blanche is the model for the violently pious Boer, Breedt, and in *The Indoor Boy* one of the main characters is an AWB disciple.

How to explain this fascination? Is it the same instinct which motivates some rape victims to seek out their violators? Or one of Dennis Nilsen's surviving victims to become pen pals with him in prison? Defying logic, we become transfixed by the monsters in our lives. We shower these villains with the kind of obsessive interest that we should reserve for our heroes.

When I watch Terre'Blanche I'm aware of his physical details, as though he were someone that I fancied. In repose, he has an animal's weight and rhythm – both lazy and dangerous. His shockingly blue eyes have this quality as well. Some people who met Hitler said he had a way of looking through you, or making you feel you weren't there. Other people said that the bones of his own face seemed to melt, and you were left gazing into this nightmarish pulp.

Terre'Blanche's greatest strength, like Hitler's, is his oratory. His voice sounds as though it comes up from the very earth of South Africa: rich, deep, baked at the edges. He also has Hitler's gift of losing himself in his words. His audiences don't get a politician's structured performance; they get a man shaking with rage and grief, pouring with sweat, ready to spill his blood as well – anything, anything for the Fatherland.

Terre'Blanche is my sworn enemy. But, as an actor, how can I fail to admire his charisma and conviction? As a writer, how can I not interest myself in the history of his people (persecuted by the British)? And as a Jew, how can I not notice that the Boers think of themselves as a Chosen People? They have a 'covenant' with the Lord, and their leading churchmen were able to root apartheid for much of its lifetime in the Bible. Terre'Blanche himself is quick to point out that the AWB emblem is not a swastika at all, but the three holy sevens from the Book of Revelation.

Terre'Blanche is driven by a sense of God within him. I'm reminded of the row when Field Marshal von Rundstedt resigned from Hitler's army. 'It's all very well for *you*,' shouted the Führer, 'but I can't go to my superior, God Almighty, and say, "I'm not carrying on with this!"'

I played Hitler recently, in the shape of Brecht's Arturo Ui. The play ends with Ui high on a Nuremberg-type podium, whipping up the faithful, and it took me a long time to admit that I loved playing this scene. I had been haunted by Hitler for so long (and by his offspring: Terre'Blanche, Le Pen, the British neo-Nazis, and so on) that it was horribly liberating to climb inside his skin at last and see the world from his point of view: a dizzy perspective across a crowd of faces craning upwards, with expressions of disgust, fascination and helplessness. 'We were glad we were not being asked to vote,' people told me afterwards. 'Glad because it would've been hard not to vote for Ui!'

It is hard to resist these people. They're like an elemental force, a magnet drawing out buried things within us all. We try to laugh them off. Hitler was dismissed as a Chaplin lookalike, and recently Nick Broomfield made a hilarious documentary on Terre'Blanche, *The Leader, His Driver and the Driver's Wife*, in which the Leader was shown having petulant tantrums, and failing to control his horse during a parade.

But we'd be fools to underestimate Terre'Blanche. Apartheid is far from dead, and civil war has not necessarily been averted by De Klerk's referendum. One man's villain is another man's hero, and for Terre'Blanche's followers (many of whom are in the police force and Army) he represents a God-given right, something they're ready to die for. It's there, chillingly, in the translation of his name: White Earth.

JOHN SIMPSON

$\Diamond$

General Vidal

11 December 1993

*John Simpson, Foreign Affairs Editor of the
BBC, on his hero, General Antonio Vidal,
who was responsible for bringing to trial
the leader of the Shining Path guerrillas*

Until a year ago, my views about the most admirable figures in any society were strictly conventional. I regarded Vaclav Havel and Andrei Sakharov as the paradigm: people who had the courage to sacrifice their everyday, comfortable existence for the principles of freedom and decency. Then I visited Peru, and realised that there might be room within the paradigm for other forms of nobility: that, however unlikely it might seem, even a secret policeman could become a hero if the circumstances were right.

Peru is Looking-Glass land, where the Vice-President says the President is in league with drug-runners, where the upholders of law and order can become seriously rich through smuggling cocaine, where the black-market rate for the dollar is lower than the official rate, and where the Maoist group Shining Path, the world's nastiest guerrilla movement, seemed capable, until last year, of taking over the government. In a country like that, a secret police chief could turn out to be the best defender of the rule of law.

It was the job of General Antonio Ketin Vidal Herrera, head of the National Anti-Terrorist Directorate, to combat Shining Path and catch its charismatic leader, Abimael Guzman. By the middle of 1992, ministers talked gloomily of a Shining Path government within months. General Vidal, small, precise and thoughtful, not at all the medal-hung, macho figure of our imaginings, was the one man who could stop it happening. He could, of course, have used torture as his instrument for hunting Guzman; other sections of Peru's convoluted security apparatus used violence instinctively. Vidal preferred a more rigorous approach: his men followed up leads, shadowed contacts, put two and two together and traced his man to a house in the moderately expensive Lima suburb of Surquillo.

So, after twelve years of ferocious guerrilla war, Guzman was trapped. Vidal's instructions were clear. They came from the most powerful man in Peru: Vladimiro Montesinos, a convicted spy-turned-lawyer who once defended big drug-runners and senior military men accused of human-rights offences, and who is now President Fujimori's chief adviser on security. He is an extraordinarily secretive figure: only one photograph of him is known to have been taken in the past decade, and the photographer who took it was beaten up and was lucky to have kept the negatives.

Montesinos is regarded as the man who tells the President what to do; unpleasant things could happen to people who crossed Montesinos; he had told General Vidal that, if he ever succeeded in capturing Guzman, Vidal was to keep the news secret, and to report it first to Montesinos personally; during the ensuing twenty-four hours, Montesinos would decide whether Guzman could be made to tell everything he knew, or whether he should be killed immediately.

General Vidal decided to disobey these orders. He didn't tell his political superiors what had happened; instead, he gave his men the order to raid the house. (Dressed as roadsweepers and gardeners, they had been watching it closely for days. Afterwards, the man who lived opposite told me ruefully he hadn't understood why it had become the best-kept street in Lima.) They moved in, and arrested Guzman without a struggle. Vidal greeted him politely. Afterwards, he escorted him to headquarters in his own car. That evening, the general rang one of the television stations with the news that the most wanted man in Peru was sitting in his office, a prisoner.

Montesinos was furious. He rang Vidal and asked if the news was a joke in bad taste; a curious way of reacting to a coup which would damage Shining Path irrevocably. 'Why didn't you do as you were told?' he asked Vidal. Soon afterwards, Montesinos sent one of his lieutenants round to demand that Guzman should be handed over. When that failed, the man threatened Vidal's life.

President Fujimori, who seems increasingly insignificant nowadays, was away in the provinces when the arrest took place. There was no glory for him in the news of the arrest; though when I interviewed him a few days later he claimed to have known that the arrest was imminent. The untruth seemed to diminish him all the more. The arrest did not destroy Shining Path: it has continued its murderous campaign. But it now lacks the subtle brain and leadership of the man who created it. With Guzman in charge, it was conceivable that Shining Path might come to power and establish a Maoist Year Zero in Peru; without him, it has been reduced to the level of a dangerous but containable guerrilla group. It will not overthrow the government now. The arrest caused huge relief in Peru, yet Vidal received relatively little attention. He certainly didn't seek it.

In safeguarding the rule of law, General Vidal had made an enemy of the most powerful figure in the country, and had wrecked his own career. When I met him, a few days afterwards, he clearly felt it had been worthwhile. 'I am doing things as they should be done,' he said quietly. Later, as neat and self-effacing as a hero from a detective story, General Vidal was awarded a middle-ranking decoration and given a new job. The saviour of his country is nowadays in charge of police personnel.

JOAN SMITH

◇

Lord Young

23 June 1990

*The feminist thriller-writer Joan Smith
is affronted by 'Mrs Thatcher's creature',
Lord Young of Graffham*

I have never met Lord Young of Graffham. For all I know he is an exceptionally kind, cultivated man who spends his spare time mucking out in his local donkey sanctuary. Perhaps he likes nothing better of an evening than to curl up with the latest novel by Muriel Spark or Ian McEwan. His *Who's Who* entry, though, presents a different picture. Lord Young plays golf. He is a solicitor. He is keen on computers.

Grey men do not come much greyer than this. There is something about those horrible double-breasted suits, always worn with the buttons done up, which suggests a buttoned-up personality – I cannot picture Lord Young wiping away a tear in a darkened cinema, let alone weeping over the pathetic human bundles visible any night on certain London streets. The homeless of Britain's cities are the products of eleven years of government by Mrs Thatcher, and Lord Young is, above all else, Mrs Thatcher's creature. He is her Frankenstein's monster, owing his political career to her in a way that has never been true of the Tebbits, the Howes or the Heseltines of this world.

His appointment as Minister without Portfolio in 1984 was an affront to democracy, made possible only by his simultaneous elevation to the House of Lords, a wheeze previously used by Harold Wilson in order to allow the *Times* journalist Alun Gwynne Jones, now the right-wing Lord Chalfont, to serve as a Foreign Office minister. Young, like Chalfont, was a man who had never submitted himself to the electorate and a minister whose decisions could not be directly questioned by MPs. Promotion quickly followed: Lord Young, who had previously supplied funds for and done a stint as Director of Mrs Thatcher's beloved Centre for Policy Studies, found himself first Secretary of State for Employment, then in charge of the Department of Trade and Industry.

Say I was an MP whose constituent, an old age pensioner, had lost her entire savings in the Barlow Clowes scandal – an investment company licensed by the DTI. Could I get up in Parliament and question the minister about the affair? I could not. I would have had to make do with his junior, while Lord Young submitted himself to the scrutiny only of the undemocratic and overwhelmingly Conservative Upper Chamber. Lord Young was, in effect, a politician with a constituency of one – the woman who had appointed him.

Even more extraordinary is the fact that he was unashamed of her patronage. 'I am the Prime Minister's foot soldier,' he said in 1987. 'I do as she wishes.' He was, he said, 'the most loyal man in the Cabinet, because as a peer I could never hope to challenge the Prime Minister. I'm out of the parliamentary rat-race. I exist only to serve her and the country.' Since the country's demands are rather harder to discern, and certainly more heterogeneous, than those of Mrs Thatcher, it is easy to imagine what this meant in practice. An *Observer* profile last year suggested that in rows with Norman Tebbit he would say, 'We are here for one person – for her. If these are what she wants, then these are what she gets.' Such toadying seems more appropriate to a sidekick of one of the horrible old dictators of Eastern Europe than a senior member of government in a democratic country.

Even if members of the public were disgusted by Young's fawning they could not vote him out at the next election. That he was aware of his invulnerability emerged when he was questioned by journalists, his demeanour frequently suggesting impatience with the notion that he should have to deal with them at all. His impatience surfaced again when, after leaving the government, he was invited to give evidence to the House of Commons Public Accounts Committee. The subject was the Rover deal, and facts had emerged which posed serious questions about his judgement. His department had concealed millions of pounds of 'sweeteners' to British Aerospace to persuade it to buy the car company; in conflict with its own stated intention of 'striving to keep markets open and free and maintain a strong competition policy', the DTI had granted BAe the sole right to negotiate, then sold Rover at a knock-down price without a full assessment of its assets. It was this latter point which interested the committee, but the invitation was brusquely refused; the PAC is unable to order the attendance of a peer. Lord Young did condescend to give evidence to the Select Committee on Trade and Industry, where he denounced criticism of the Rover sale as 'disgraceful' and described it as the 'deal of the decade'.

Now that Lord Young has retired from politics to spend more time with his business interests – his appointment as executive chairman of Cable & Wireless, a major beneficiary of his former department's privatisation policy, was announced last week – the memorials to his nearly five years of public office are writ large. For a man obsessed with a mission to run government like big business, there is a pleasing irony in the fact they include a series of company names: Rover, Harrods, Barlow Clowes – monumental cock-ups every one.

RALPH STEADMAN

◇

Franz Anton Mesmer

3 July 1993

*Ralph Steadman praises the heroic
persistence of the quack doctor*

Franz Anton Mesmer, a physician born in Austria in 1734, is my hero because he was such a charlatan. I have modelled my life on his.

Mesmer claimed to have found a way of curing illnesses by means of the magnetism peculiar to animal bodies, and, most noticeably, peculiar to Mesmer himself. To effect a cure he would fix his intense green eyes upon the patients, glare at them meaningfully, and take their money. Mesmer 'mesmerised' them.

His theory was that the heavenly bodies exercise an influence on organic bodies, animals and humans alike, by means of an invisible fluid diffusing itself through the universe like plasma. He insisted that diseases could be cured by harnessing the magnetism swirling all around.

There was no shortage of gullible patients, but Mesmer's attempts to be recognised by the medical establishment met with derision. And in the late 1750s, when he failed to cure Mademoiselle Paradis, a blind Viennese pianist, he was denounced by Austrian scientists. His experiments had left Mlle Paradis apoplectic and tone deaf, though, in Mesmer's defence, it must be said that music lovers who had heard her play before the operation said she was tone deaf anyway.

Mesmer quit Vienna for Paris in 1778. His rampant self-esteem unabated, he demanded that in return for his scientific research the French government present him with a château and an estate. A hypochondriacal baron offered to back him, but only if Mesmer would agree to set up a 'magnetic clinic' where the doctor could train officials, picked by the baron, in his mysterious methods.

Mesmer turned down this offer, perhaps fearing exposure, but in 1784 he agreed, in exchange for honours and money, to subject his claims to a committee of physicians and the French Academy of Sciences.

With the help of one of his patients, a compliant woman suffering from little more than a desire to go on the stage, Mesmer demonstrated his methods of animal magnetism as follows:

'Gentlemen, with only my hands I touch and stroke the patient. I breathe on him and fix my eyes upon him. The magnetised person must always be of a weaker constitution and, if possible, a different sex from the magnetiser [*woman goes limp*], otherwise the magnetiser will suffer a severe loss of power in the nervous system. The patient must also believe without doubting [*woman nods earnestly*].

'The phenomenon he experiences consists of bodily sensations resulting in chilliness, heaviness, flying pains and oppressions, and a diminishing activity of the eternal senses. He will faint [*woman faints on to nearby ottoman*], experience convulsions [*she writhes about embarrassingly*], and sleep with lively dreams [*woman: "Ooh! Ahh! Ooh! Ooh! Away! Begone!"*]. I call this "magnetic sleep".

'The magnetised person is now transported to higher spheres, gentlemen, and observes the internal organisation of his own body. He receives inspired news of Heaven, Hell and Purgatory, and reads sealed letters laid on his stomach [*woman, seized by stage fright, forgets her lines and fails to reveal the contents of the letters*]. He now perceives the presence of disbelievers and has a fit. Hence, gentlemen, it is necessary to keep sceptics at a distance in order to witness this highest of human phenomena.

'When the patient awakes he will be unconscious of what he has experienced, and therefore cannot tell you what I know to be true [*woman's eyes open and she begs for water*].'

The committee decreed that animal magnetism was a futile exercise and Mesmer a dismal quack. Disgusted, more by the woman's performance than by his humiliating dismissal, Mesmer left for England that year, where he tried unsuccessfully to persuade the populace of his supernatural powers. He died a frustrated man, in 1815.

Mesmer's persistence was heroic – and, in spite of his bogus practices, he was charming and colourful; he still is mesmerising.

D. J. TAYLOR

The Singing Postman

26 February 1994

*The novelist and critic on Allan
Smethurst, the Singing Postman,
who was the authentic voice
of rural Norfolk*

The Sixties threw up some unlikely pop stars. There was Wee Willie Harris, with his frothy, empurpled hair; Pinky and Perky (before the inevitable split over 'musical differences'); ensembles with names like the 1910 Fruitgum Co. Set against the pageant of genuine weirdness that, a quarter of a century ago, paraded through the average front room each Thursday on *Top of the Pops*, Mr Blobby is but a pale and decadent shadow. The most implausible of all – yet more appealing in that he came not from Liverpool or Manchester but from my own juvenile romping ground of Norfolk – was a character called the Singing Postman.

Oddly enough, he really was, or had been, a postman – there were publicity shots of him setting out on his rounds on an elderly push-bike, and the peaked GPO-issue cap, perched above dense aquarium spectacles, never left his head. The Singing Postman's real name was Allan Smethurst, and with his orthodontically challenged grin and his Woolworth's guitar, he cruised effortlessly through the stagnant waters of mid-Sixties Norfolk, in and out of the pages of the *Eastern Daily Press*, and on towards the glamorous harbours of *Nationwide* and the *Des O'Connor Show*. I still have a tape of his classic late-Sixties album *The Singing Postman's Year*, though only collectors can afford to fight over his EPs, with their lesser-known tracks 'Oi Can't Git a Noice Loaf of Bread!' and 'A Miss from Diss!'.

Twenty-five years on, and without the help of a tape recorder, it is hard to convey what the Singing Postman sounded like. To call him a yokel George Formby is tempting, but inaccurate. Folk poetry set to music is nearer the mark, but still not quite there. The songs themselves are impossibly stylised: limping guitar accompaniment, drowned out by a jaunty, quavering tenor that is clearly having trouble with its 'r's. There was a famous signature tune, 'Hev Yew Gotta Loight, Boy?', that still lurks unbidden in the memory of anyone over thirty brought up in Norfolk. An account of a relationship with a chain-smoking girlfriend, this contains the immortal refrain:

> Molly Windley, she smoke like a chimbley
> but she's my little nicotine gal.

There are dozens more in the same vein: 'Suffin' cold' ('Oh my lor', tha's suffin' cold'), 'Are Yew Alroight, Boy?' ('Oi wear horned-rimmed glasses'). At their most basic level the songs are simply a repository for Norfolk dialect, intricate rural speech patterns put into rhyming couplets, as in the opening lines to 'Hev Yew Gotta Loight, Boy?':

> I know a gal, real nice gal, down in Wroxham way
> She were wholly nice to me, back in the old school days.

It is the 'wholly' (pronounced 'hully') that makes it authentic, a reproduction of the way in which Norfolk people actually speak rather than a fragment of yokel parody. Yet for all the jauntiness and the dialect jokes about 'When I tried to howd her close/she says "Now howd you hard"', it is an edgy, doleful type of comedy. In fact, the Singing Postman's repertoire is a kind of elegy to a lost age.

Born in the mid-Twenties at Sheringham, on the Norfolk coast, he moved to Grimsby during the War: most of the songs, consequently, look back on a bygone Norfolk childhood ('I'm always thinking of a seaside town, and wishing I wor there'), legends like Black Shuck, the ghostly hound of the beaches ('We all know Shuck, he's a real ol' dawg'), the vanished summers of 'Followin' the boinder round'.

Fame gestured briefly in the mid-Sixties when 'Hev Yew Gotta Loight, Boy?' achieved national airplay. Somehow, amid the follow-ups, the tours and the spending of a fair amount of money, it all went sour. Towards the end of the decade, the records dried up (despite late-period classics like 'They're Orl Playin' Dommies [dominoes] in the Bar') and there was a nasty court appearance on an assault charge involving his mother and stepfather. By this time, too, curling fingers were threatening his guitar-playing. In 1970, after an unsuccessful operation, he quit the music business, as the trade papers say, for good.

'Hev Yew Gotta Loight, Boy?' turned up on television recently, when an inspired creative director decided to use it in an advertisement for Ovaltine Light. Reporters managed to track Allan down, back in Grimsby and living in a Salvation Army hostel. Now in his late sixties, he said he would be 'satisfied with anything they give me' – the advertisement is expected to bring him about £2,000 in royalties. His expenses were modest, he added, but he supposed he might spend the money on clothes. The Salvation Army captain thought no one had visited him for seven years.

It is all terribly sad, but somehow in keeping with the songs, which are wistful affairs, full of longing for a world which was disappearing even as he sang about it, a clotted and mostly roseate universe of following the combines over wheatfields in the fag-end of summer, watching the crab-boats set out, taking rattletrap trains into Norwich for the winter sales. The Singing Postman is gone now, gone along with the old Norwich cattle market and the Gaumont cinema; but I salute a man who seems as much a part of my childhood as Great Yarmouth funfair or the boats drawn up on the Sheringham shale.

ROSE TREMAIN

◇

Angus Wilson

19 May 1990

*Rose Tremain was horrified by the neglect
of her friend, hero and fellow-novelist, the
late Sir Angus Wilson*

The first writer I ever met was Angus Wilson. I met him at the University of East Anglia in 1964, the year he published his fifth novel, *Late Call*. My copy of this book is bound with one of those transparent plastic covers bookshops used to sell in the days before glossy jackets. They cost 9d each and I only ever put them on books I sensed I would cherish. *Late Call* is a cherished book. I admire it and treasure it not only because I believe it is Angus's masterpiece (in which his powers of mimicry and satire and his skill as a female portraitist combine to create a moving yet acerbic story about goodness) but also because to hold the book in my hands is to be reminded of that meeting and the twenty-five years of friendship that have followed it.

Angus's generosity of spirit, very apparent in his fiction, has always manifested itself in acts of generosity, both spiritual and material. That part of his nature that responds so passionately to Dickens has made him not merely an acute observer of all kinds and types and classes of people, but has also allowed him to be truly interested in their destinies. The help he has given to younger writers has been one important manifestation of this interest. To me, a young writer with, as yet, no coherent vision, he gave not only time and practical help but also something of himself, telling anecdotes about his South African childhood, about the writing of his first short story, 'Raspberry Jam', about people he knew, about his love for his garden. And in that garden in Suffolk, he and Tony Garrett gave an annual summer party that had, in retrospect, something of a pre-War insouciance about it. The sun always shone. Tony poured champagne. The garden was full of old-fashioned flowers. Angus, resplendent in a purple bow tie and a white suit, was like a magnet, drawing everybody to him.

He talked of Paris or Iowa or Sri Lanka, of his old foe Jack Priestley, or his old neighbour and friend Freddie Ashton, of visits to Clarence House or fund-raising efforts for his local theatre. There was a great deal of laughter. We drove home drunk. I remember longing for a year to pass so that another such day would come around.

As a novelist, Angus has taught me a great many things. He taught me how vital it is for writers to read and re-read widely and consistently. He read all the novels of Dickens, Jane Austen and George Eliot every two or three years. As frequently he would re-read his favourite novels by Waugh, Lawrence, Forster, Thomas Mann and Saul Bellow. Though he stopped reviewing novels in the Fifties because he disliked standing in judgement on his contemporaries, he followed with extreme care what his peers were doing.

He taught me to take risks, to resist petrification, to try to chart in each successive book new territory, to be sceptical about what one has achieved so far. His writings on the work of Ivy Compton Burnett reveal succinctly his belief that the writer whose work does not demonstrate an inner development, a gradual unconscious change, will never be regarded as a great writer. Of Compton Burnett he says, 'Her novels remain the same. She presents us with a whole view of life and conveys that whole view in a subtle and convincing way, but she does not tell us more about it or show it to us from another side or make us think or feel about it more deeply that she did from the very start.'

Angus's own works, however, show us a writer engaged in a heroic quest to show us the familiar and the unfamiliar 'from another side'. The cast of Angus's fiction is huge and the protagonists of his last novel, *Setting the World on Fire*, struggle with the conflicting forces of individualism and society, order and disorder in ways unimaginable to those of *Hemlock and After*, his first.

His work has underlined for me two other important considerations. He admired Dickens and Dostoevsky above all other novelists for 'their extraordinary mixture of black and comic vision which allowed them to see how profound absurdity can be and how utterly ridiculous most of the profound things often are'. A deep understanding of the way the comic illuminates the tragic pervades his own work, and I now perceive that almost all the writers I most admire possess this gift in some measure. Perhaps most importantly of all, Angus's ability to write convincingly about – and from the point of view of – women has confirmed my view that it is possible in fiction to transcend sex and gender and to address life from that elusive 'other side' to which one has only secondary access. For why not? The country of the imagination is rich and vast. Writers should surely not be tourists there, but rather explorers and mountaineers.

Angus is now seventy-six and gravely ill. He will write no more books. He lives in a nursing home near Bury St Edmunds. His novels no longer sell widely and Tony struggles to find the money to pay the nursing-home bills. Has the world forgotten what a great writer Angus Wilson was and what a distinguished and heroic life he led? It seems as if it has. Try as I may, I can find no comedy in this.

AUBERON WAUGH

◇

Pamella Bordes

30 September 1989

Pamella Bordes, 'a most uncommon
prostitute', displaced the Princess of Wales
as the object of Auberon Waugh's adulation

Pamella Bordes may be aware that she has a certain amount in common with the Princess of Wales. They are the same age – Pamella is the elder by just six weeks – and both, in their different ways, show a certain aptitude for social advancement. The Princess of Wales was born on the same day that I, a child bridegroom, walked up the aisle of the Church of Our Lady and the Assumption in Warwick Street. Pamella, six weeks old at the time and living in the remote north of India, was just limbering up for her first major setback, when her father, Major Mohinder Singh Chaudhery, was killed in a clash on the border between China and India.

Perhaps it is essential to the nature of true hero-worship that we should never meet our heroes. Another thing that the Princess of Wales and Pamella Bordes have in common, although they may not be aware of it, is that neither has ever met me. Nor, I fear, would it be a matter of the slightest interest to either of them to learn that after nearly eight years of hero-worshipping the Princess of Wales with a pure and distant passion, I found in March of this year that her pedestal was now occupied by the shorter, plumper, browner figure of Madam Bordes.

Perhaps it was the same quality of pluck or daring which first excited my admiration for both women, although in the case of the princess the thing which finally made me her slave was the discovery that she had got where she was with only one O level, in domestic science. What destroyed my passion was when somebody told me she was a fanatical anti-smoker and would not allow anyone to smoke in her presence. Possibly this was a vile calumny. I shall almost certainly never know. But already Pamella was edging her way up the side of the pedestal when somebody pointed her out to me at a literary party and said she was the person who, towards the end of an affair with Andrew Neil, the Editor of the *Sunday Times*, had cut the gussets from the trousers of all his ghastly suits.

I don't think there would be any problem about smoking in Pamella's company. Although I believe she is a vegetarian, that is not always an unattractive thing in a young woman. At the height of her brief, halcyon moment of glory, she told the *Daily Mail*'s Lynda Lee-Potter how she looked her men up in *Who's Who*, researched their interests and tried to take up those interests herself: 'If he rides, then I ride. If he shoots, then I shoot. If he likes the ballet, then I take up the ballet.' Using these and other wiles at which we can only guess, Pamella pulled herself up by her bootlaces to a point where she was known and accepted and liked by rich and famous people in London, Paris, Washington and New York, not to mention Tripoli and points east.

Nervous and priggish people who dismiss her as a common prostitute are quite wrong. She was a most uncommon prostitute. It is as much as your average English prostitute can do to catch a train from Liverpool to King's Cross. After she had left her family behind to become Miss India and take Washington by storm, she was completely on her own, picking up what friends she could along the way, with nothing but her own beauty, charm and extraordinary courage to see her through.

My hero-worship, then, is for a person who can suffer the most appalling, unimaginable indignities and still come through smiling. One shudders to think what she must have had to put up with privately from Arab sheiks, arms dealers, American bankers and others who comprise the clientele of a plucky girl on the make from nowhere – not to mention Murdoch's lackey Andrew Neil, 'editor of the most powerful newspaper in the world'. There is not a hint of bitterness or self-pity in anything she has written or said about her experiences, and scarcely an element of kiss-and-tell. She is a true professional – the equivalent, in her line of business, of Henry Moore or Richard Rogers or Rupert Murdoch in theirs.

Her destruction was brought about by two sneaks posing as reporters from Murdoch's *News of the World* who offered her Murdoch money for sexual favours and then plastered her acceptance all over that stinking newspaper. At the height of her glory, as Neil's mistress, she lunched with Murdoch and his wife (by the account she related to Lynda Lee-Potter at any rate). After the *News of the World* exposed her, Murdoch's *Today* pursued her with a vicious account of her life and times, calculated finally to destroy her livelihood in her own or any other profession.

It is no good pretending that her brief, kingfisher appearance on the national scene scaled quite the heights reached by others. An affair with Andrew Neil, a dance with Colin Moyni-han, Minister of Sport, and a curious, inconclusive drink in the bedroom of Captain Mark Phillips, do not quite add up to an alliance with the heir to the throne. But coming from nowhere, she did her best. Goodness knows where she is now, or what she is doing, but wherever she is and whatever she is doing, I wish her luck.

JOHN WELLS

◇
────────────────────────────────

Joan Littlewood

29 February 1992

*The actor and writer celebrates the
magical genius of the theatre director
Joan Littlewood*

Joan Littlewood is, and always has been, a brilliant clown: she once played a comic maid for Laurel and Hardy. I've never forgotten a live interview she did on the BBC's old *Tonight* programme, where she pushed her little woolly hat further and further back on her head until it fell down behind the studio chair, entirely, I am sure, so that she could turn round and retrieve it, kneeling on the seat and thrusting her bottom into the camera, to the great discomfiture of the interviewer, for what seemed like several minutes.

But her genius is as a theatre director. Theatre directors have to be witch-doctors, mediums, magicians: whether the playwright is alive or long-dead, the director has to re-create, from a very minimal top line – the written dialogue – a whole invisible, unrecorded score. Not only how characters speak, but how they look, how they look at each other, how they watch each other, how they think, think about each other, how they feel, feel about each other, how they move, alone or together, and when. The few stage directions apart, none of that is in the script.

If that whole interrelated world comes alive, the miracle happens: the playwright's dream floats free in the collective imagination of the audience.

Unlike most directors, Joan Littlewood set out to serve the author. Her technique contained a certain element of mumbo-jumbo. There was always, on the first morning of rehearsals, an introductory talk about the play, delivered in a haze of cigarette smoke; her long fingers tracing graceful patterns through it, hooded eyes focused on another world. She threw in references to contemporary politics, dreadful obscenities – filmed interviews with her often had to be bleeped two or three times a sentence – bits of gossip, mention of 'those crazy cats in Ben Jonson's day', of a vanished golden age of untrammelled sexual indulgence, of untutored genius, of the truth of a gesture, of the need for delicacy, for sensitivity, for grace.

Few of those listening had a blind idea what she was talking about, but she wove the spell. The company was hooked, under the influence. They loved it.

Then followed the analysis of the text, which they liked less: not just your own lines, everybody's lines. This involved collectively breaking the play down into units, finding the 'active verb': we know what they're *saying*, what are they *doing*?

Her greatest gift is and always has been for extraordinary sensitivity, for unlocking inhibitions: people who had never spoken before told stories, offered suggestions and identified hidden conflicts – often in themselves. She taught. These conversations went on for a long time, and when the play opened it showed: everything was illuminated from within by a shared intelligence and insight.

The improvisations contributed, too. Actors had to abandon the script and find 'parallels'. It seemed like a game. Many people hated it and complained they were wasting rehearsal time. How much space do you give to a big newspaper proprietor in a television studio? How do you have lunch alone with someone you suspect is having an affair with your wife? The players made it up, made each other laugh, frightened or surprised each other, sometimes themselves. Then they played the original scene, and it was almost always deeper and more secure.

If the players hated that, they hated one other thing a great deal more. Everyone had to read a book about some aspect of the play and give a lecture on it: if the play was set in

Aden, give a slide show on local pottery. One old French actor in Paris, in the middle of some such lantern lecture about tribal art in Katanga, sprang to his feet, camouflage-lit by the projector, shouted, 'Madame Leettlewood, hi ham han hactor, hi weesh to re-earse!' and walked out.

Very late in the rehearsal schedule, she added 'the feet'. The play was blocked, powerful positions on the stage occupied. She danced the moves, making 'floor patterns', and later watched them critically throughout the run from the dress circle: the course the weak steered round the strong, the loops and swirls of thieves in a crowd, the flow of lovers walking on a summer evening. The lines sounded equally inevitable, equally true.

By the time the show opened, the actors were so soaked in the play that they could turn upstage and the audience could smell their emotions. Littlewood calls it a 'chemical reaction'.

If a great deal of this seems familiar from any description of modern rehearsal techniques, it is because Littlewood's influence on British theatre today is universal, if almost universally unacknowledged.

Joan Littlewood always was, and still is, a beautiful, wistful clown, incapable of an unoriginal thought, an inelegant gesture. Theatre for her has never been confined to the stage, it's some kind of mystical definition of what happens when people watch other people and see themselves, a generator of innocent joy.

She has refused to direct a show for the past twenty years. I wish she'd come back and teach us.

EDMUND WHITE

◇

James Merrill

19 June 1993

*The author on his hero, the poet,
playwright and novelist James Merrill*

My first meeting with James Merrill was far from auspicious. I was introduced to him by a mutual friend, the literary critic David Kalstone, who revered him because he was America's greatest poet (and the person who had injected glamour into his life). I read to Merrill the first chapter of my first novel and he said absolutely nothing. On the way home I considered stepping out in front of a car. That was in 1971.

The funny thing is that Jimmy isn't like that at all. He's very generous with praise unless he detests something, then he's at least polite, because he has the most exquisite manners in the world. Perhaps he assumed I didn't care for comments; after all, I didn't look like a beginner. I was already thirty-one years old.

Of course I cared very much, since, for me, he was the only living writer who recalled, even rivalled, Proust – the same grasp of social nuance, the same knack for gliding seamlessly through melismatic wordplay from *mondanités* to metaphysics – although he was a lot funnier than Proust.

Just as André Gide had rejected *Swann's Way* without reading it, because he assumed a snob such as Proust couldn't write anything except spicy gossip or tepid flattery, some of Merrill's first critics had assumed that this boy, born, in 1926, with a mouthful of silver spoon (his father founded Merrill Lynch, the world's largest brokerage house), wouldn't be able to write anything but bejewelled society verse. Merrill's triumph was that, without surrendering that tone – satiric, melancholy, frivolous – he was able to tackle all the big questions.

This same contrast of the silly and the serious is what makes him such an inspiring friend. He's the person I turned to when David Kalstone died of Aids. Jimmy has a poet's sense of ceremony, though he's never sanctimonious, and when he mixed David's ashes with the ashes of a poem he'd written to him and swirled them into a tidal river in Connecticut, the act was made authentic by Jimmy's genuine pantheism.

When he reads, his voice is a tender, expressive instrument, but in conversation he has a maddening Mandarin drawl, a mix of his mother's Southern accent, a long-forgotten New England boarding-school dialect and some mid-Atlantic invention of his own. His taste in clothes reminds me why in French the adjective 'original' is usually disapproving. He can take an implacable dislike to perfectly decent (or ordinarily indecent) people.

Those are his faults. His virtues are a belief in beauty; a gift for friendship; an impertinent, punning wit in the face of tragedy; fidelity in love; and a stern discipline in making his art. While those around him are dying or going gaga or checking back into rehab, he continues to write – not as the unfeeling monster of egotism he once feared he'd become, but as the golden voice for so much leaden pain.

After a loss of my own, I telephoned Jimmy in New York from Paris the other day and asked him how we keep going on. 'We're tough as nails,' he said, which is both observation and exhortation.

He is my hero because he writes as though the world were full of cultured, funny people who have read all the books but are far from sad about the flesh. There aren't many people on the look-out for mere truth, beauty and goodness, nor do they know to look in the ragtime and bone-china shop of Merrill's verse, but no matter. JM never repeats himself, never writes an ugly line or false word, and he gives to every poem a high finish and a ravishing spin.

He once said that what he learned from Wallace Stevens,

Elizabeth Bishop and W. H. Auden was that a writer doesn't have to lead a 'literary' life in a ghetto of 'creativity'. Bishop, in particular, showed him the value of a daily life with a 'random, Chekhovian surface, open to trivia and funny surprises, or even painful ones, today a fit of weeping, tomorrow a picnic'. Merrill, in turn, has taught me that 'amateur' is just another word for the lover of personal freedom and the quirky freelance sensibility.

NIGEL WILLIAMS

P. G. Wodehouse

6 April 1991

*The novelist and playwright Nigel
Williams finds a heroic ideal in
P. G. Wodehouse's ability to disappear
into his own fictional world*

There is nothing immediately heroic about P. G. Wodehouse. Apart from a brief and undistinguished career as a bank clerk, he spent most of his long life writing some of the best comic novels written this century. And, although I admire him greatly as a prose stylist (as Tom Sharpe has pointed out, anyone who can write a simile like 'She had a laugh like a troop of cavalry going over a tin bridge' is well worth watching), I am normally of the opinion that writers shouldn't make heroes of other writers. It always smacks of those athletes telling you which fizzy drink they like. But there is a quality in Wodehouse the man that is most definitely of heroic proportions. I glimpsed it first in the early Seventies, when I watched a BBC interview with him at his home in Long Island.

The interviewer devoted at least half of his time to asking Wodehouse questions about his wartime broadcasts. Wodehouse had been living in Le Touquet at the start of the Second World War and was unable to get back to Britain. He was interned in Germany, and then released in 1940 on grounds of age (he was by then sixty). Trapped in Berlin, he gave a series of humorous, non-political broadcasts on German radio with the intention of reassuring his American fans as to his safety. These harmless pieces were monitored by the BBC listening service, and, thanks to the Minister of Information, Duff Cooper, became a hot political issue. Wodehouse was branded as a Fascist, which he wasn't.

Thirty years on, it was a subject which obviously made him very uncomfortable, and the line of questioning, designed chiefly to elicit his feelings on the issue rather than to clarify the facts of the case, did nothing to make the old boy look any happier. The pauses between question and response grew longer and longer until, at the last question, 'Do you still think of yourself as an Englishman?', Wodehouse looked long and hard at his knees, and then off to the right, for about ten seconds before replying. 'I suppose I do . . .' was his response, and after he'd said that he looked away into the distance as if in the hope that some other chap would come haring up the drive with the kind of response the BBC might consider satisfactory. They had left the camera running on his silence, and that was how the film ended, with an image of an old man, broken and betrayed by the England he had written about so well.

But there was something about that image that puzzled me. I wouldn't have said there was a heroic quality to his silence but I wanted to know more, and, with the intention of penetrating that reserve, I found myself nearly twenty years later making a biography of Wodehouse for the BBC. As I trailed from survivor to survivor, almost the only firm impression I managed to gain was that he was extremely shy. Once, apparently, when his wife was off to buy an apartment in New York, he said to her, 'Make sure you get one on the ground floor.' 'Why?' she asked, and he replied, 'I can never think of what to say to the liftman . . .'

People referred to his genuine innocence, his unhappy childhood or his kindness and gentleness in human relations, but I never really felt they had known the man about whom they were talking. It was as if the man I was pursuing wasn't really there at all. Some people told us about the 'Wodehouse glide'. If there was any danger of what his sister-in-law Nella Wodehouse called an 'atmosphere', he would trickle from the room, rather as Jeeves trickled into Bertie's bedroom after his master had had a particularly hard night. The Wodehouse *oeuvre* is full of words that describe characters trickling or gliding away from rooms where things are getting sticky, and it was as if the old master of farce had performed this same trick on us.

Puzzled, I went back to that BBC footage. There was the old man in the garden. There were the questions, and there, once again, was Wodehouse looking off into the distance for what seemed an age. Except, now, I wasn't so sure that this silence masked a deep grief about his exile. After running the film about fifteen times the editor and I decided he looked positively cheerful. I went back to the interviews I had filmed, and, in the transcript of a conversation with his biographer, Frances Donaldson, I found the clue that both unlocked his characters and began, for me, the realisation that there was something heroic about him. 'He wasn't', Lady Donaldson had said, 'really there at all. He spent nearly all his waking life in the company of Jeeves and Bertie Wooster. And that was where he belonged.' She was right. The man had disappeared into his work, and there are very, very few writers good enough, or self-effacing enough about the craft of fiction, to be able to do that. His isolated, impassioned pursuit of a fictional world that to a man as clever and well-read as he was must have often seemed irrelevant or absurd (it is very important not to confuse Wodehouse with Wooster) presents all serious writers, especially those who dare to make jokes, with an ideal that can only be described by the word 'heroic'.

A. N. WILSON

---◊---

Jesus

19 September 1992

A. N. Wilson, biographer of Christ,
explains why a Jesus stripped of religion
remains his hero

Jesus is my hero, not my god. Publishers like the word 'controversial', and my book on Jesus has been labelled 'controversial', which nearly always means 'offensive'. I did not write about Jesus to denigrate him, but to see if I could rescue him from the encrustations of the Christian myth.

Thanks to the scholars who have steeped themselves in the history of first-century Judaism and in the Rabbinic texts, we now know far more than our Christian ancestors did about the sort of world Jesus inhabited, and the sort of teacher he was. He was not the only Galilean teacher and wonder-worker. Hanina Ben Dosa and Honi the Circle Drawer were, like Jesus, attributed with miraculous powers. It was believed that they could control the weather, raise up the sick, exorcise demons. At his baptism, a heavenly voice saluted Jesus as 'My beloved son!'. This happens to several holy men in the Rabbinic texts. All religions produce folklore of this kind, and it is not the miraculous doings of Jesus which really make him distinctive. Nor, even, is resurrection from the dead wholly unknown in first-century Judaism. In Matthew's Gospel alone, we read that a whole cemetery rose up, like a canvas of Stanley Spencer.

What makes Jesus unique is his teaching. He had the power to undermine everything by asking profound ethical and psychological questions. Centuries before Freud, he asked people to realise that our behaviour is not determined by conventions or superficial obedience to codes. While the Torah tells us that divorce is legal, Jesus asks his hearers to consider the deep, irrational power of lust. While the Torah forbids murder, he asks where anger comes from. He told his followers to be like little children – not like older children, but like babies, accepting life as it comes – not asking how we are clothed or where the next meal is coming from. He taught that, in order to live, human beings must learn to die, that the last will be first. The natural human pursuits of appetite and power are turned on their head in his highly original and distinctive reinterpretation of the Jewish law.

He was, of course, a Jew, and there is no evidence whatsoever that he ever wished to found a new religion. When asked to meet gentiles, he said that he had no interest in them, and – in that strong way of speaking which the Gospels fragmentarily record – he called them dogs and pigs. He could be extremely offensive. Mark's Gospel tells us that his family thought he was mad.

It is hard to know what Jesus thought about things in general, since most of his sayings, clothed in analogies of simple life (bread-making, gardening, housework), relate to the specific. Many scholars believe that Jesus thought that the world order would end in his lifetime, that the Romans would be driven out of Israel, that the Temple of Herod would be destroyed by God and replaced with the Temple of Solomon, and that a new age would be ushered in, the age of the saints, presided over by the Anointed One, the Messiah.

This did not happen. Jerusalem was destroyed by the Romans in the year 70. The Jews bravely went on being Jews. And the small group of Jewish heretics who came to be known as Christians took their beliefs to the cities of the ancient world, including Rome itself. None of this could conceivably have been in Jesus's mind when he died on the cross for causing a public disorder during Passover in or around the year 30. The fact that his ideas were disseminated in Greek by gentiles, in the Epistles of Paul, in the Gospels, and later in the Church's theology, would have angered him as much as it would have pleased him. He never claimed to be God.

The Gospels never said that he did so; and, for a monotheist such as Jesus, the idea of Christianity would have been shocking and repugnant.

But, by the accident of Christianity, Jesus changed the world. He did not address himself to groups but to individuals. Even those who were beyond the pale – prostitutes, tax collectors and political terrorists – were his friends. He had no time for religious ascetics, and was accused of being a drunkard. Because of him, the ancient world began to think the unthinkable: that slaves were human beings, as important in the eyes of God as the emperor himself.

The human race has not been quick to follow Jesus's teachings, but they remain, like a sort of delayed time bomb, embedded in the Gospels, and every so often in history, they explode. But it did not occur to many Christians that slavery was contrary to the teachings of Jesus until 1,800 years after the crucifixion. Jesus befriended women (something which the strictest Judaism of his day forbade). This did not stop Christians preaching anti-female propaganda (that sin came into the world through Eve and so on) for 1,900 years. But Socialism and feminism both owe much to Jesus.

It does not seem completely fanciful to me to believe with Pasternak that 'history as we know it began with Christ'. What, asks Pasternak, is the distinctive thing that started with Christ? 'Firstly, the love of one's neighbour – the supreme form of living energy. And secondly, the two concepts which are the make-up of any modern man . . . the ideas of free personality and of life as a sacrifice.'